D1242375

PN 4889 .A1 J56

British Children's Authors

British Children's Authors

Interviews at Home

CORNELIA JONES

and OLIVIA R. WAY

VON CANON LIBRARY
SOUTHERN SEMINARY
BUENA VISTA, VIRGINIA 24416

29542

American Library Association

Chicago 1976

Jones, Cornelia, 1921-
    British children's authors; interviews at home.
Library of Congress Cataloging in Publication Data
    Bibliography: p.
    1. Children's literature, English—History and criti-
cism. 2. Authors, English—20th century—Interviews.
3. Illustrators—Great Britain—Interviews. I. Way,
Olivia R., 1914-   joint author.   II. Title.
PN1009.A1J56   820′.9   76-44494
ISBN 0-8389-0224-3

Copyright © 1976 by the American Library Association

All rights reserved. No part of this publication may be reproduced in any form
without permission in writing from the publisher, except by a reviewer
who may quote brief passages in a review.

Printed in the United States of America

Contents

Introduction

When the Board of Education made sabbatical leaves available to the professional staff of our school system, we realized that a long hoped for dream might become a reality. Because we are elementary school librarians with an active interest in children and their books, we had long thought it would be an exciting and productive experience to see Europe and Great Britain through historical and modern children's books and their authors. With this in mind, we immediately began to plan our project and were fortunate to be granted the sabbatical to carry it out.

The children with whom we work enjoy the books of many British and European authors. Using their enjoyment as one of the criteria, we contacted authors and illustrators of stature, explained our project to them, and asked if they would favor us with an interview. For numerous reasons, it was not possible to arrange interviews with all those we originally contacted. However, we were extremely fortunate in the people we were privileged to meet.

For eight months we traveled on the Continent and through Great Britain, recording interviews with authors and illustrators and photographing the settings of many children's books. Our primary purpose was to share this material with children, teachers, and librarians in our school system. We felt that a resource of this type would add another dimension to the introduction and discussion of books with children.

When others in the field of children's literature became aware of the project, they expressed a desire to have the interviews made available to the profession. It occurred to us then that the interviews in book form might be an interesting and useful tool. As we considered the preparation of such a volume, we decided to include only those interviews with British authors and illustrators. In these interviews, each author and illustrator not only discussed his philosophy and his methods of working but also revealed something of his own culture and personality. To preserve the special character of each author's contribution, a minimum of editing has been done. It seemed that a brief biography of the author and an annotated bibliography of his works would be helpful. The bibliographies include only those books published in the United States. Titles selected are those we considered to be the best of the author's or illustrator's works for young readers. Some out-of-print titles are included because they are still in use in many library collections and continue to have appeal for children.

We believe that many people will find this publication useful. Children's librarians in school and public libraries, classroom teachers, and professors of children's literature may find these interviews add interest to their presentation of books. Young readers in search of material about a favorite author or illustrator may gain an understanding which will lead them on to further reading.

We hope that this collection of interviews with British authors and illustrators will make a worthwhile contribution to the literature about children's books.

Acknowledgments

We are grateful to the authors and illustrators who so graciously received us and made these interviews possible. Special thanks are also due the children's book editors, librarians, and others interested in children's books, both here and abroad, who gave encouragement and help as we planned and carried out our project.

As the Authors See Themselves

Joan Aiken

Joan Aiken was born in England in 1924. Her father, the American poet Conrad Aiken, and her Canadian mother settled in England two years before her birth. She is an English citizen by accident—her parents forgot to register her at the United States Embassy.

Because her family lived in a remote country village, Miss Aiken was taught at home by her mother until she was twelve. With her older brother and sister away at school and no playmates of her own age nearby, she was a solitary child. Her chief amusements were reading and going for walks, and on these walks she made up stories to entertain her younger brother and herself. With her mother, she went for walks and on picnics. Books were taken along in baskets, and mother and children sat under trees and read.

When she was seventeen, she wrote down the stories she had told her brother, and some of them were broadcast by the British Broadcasting Corporation. Her short stories and novels began to be published while she worked at a variety of other jobs. She has been a magazine editor, a copywriter for an advertising firm, and has worked in the London office of the United Nations. During this time, she married and had two children, John and Liz.

Miss Aiken lives now in the same part of the country where she grew up. It has not changed much since she was a child. She can still find the spot, she says, where David Copperfield met Mr. Murdstone.

Her home is a former pub, called the White Hart House, in the old and unspoiled village of Petworth. Most of her time is devoted to writing, but she enjoys gardening and painting and is a collector of nineteenth-century children's books.

Joan Aiken. Photograph by Lizza Aiken.

Interview

Joan Aiken has combined humor and adventure in a foursome of highly entertaining melodramas: THE WOLVES OF WIL-LOUGHBY CHASE, BLACK HEARTS IN BATTERSEA, NIGHTBIRDS ON NANTUCKET, *and* THE WHISPERING MOUNTAIN. *The perilous adventures of her dauntless heroes and heroines are told in a style which inevitably brings Charles Dickens to mind.*

I think I got the idea for writing melodrama for boys and girls because when I was young, I had a great deal of Dickens read aloud to me. Of course, he is the prime example of this kind of melodrama. I think this had a very strong influence on my writing. The historical period of *The Wolves of Willoughby Chase* and the others is imaginary, although the trappings are all fairly genuine English nineteenth-century ones. This again, I think, was heavily influenced by Dickens. It seems to me that this imaginary period lent itself very well to my purposes because it had features which are part of today's life, such as trains. I think children enjoy this sort of thing—things that are familiar. But it also had unlimited scope for melodrama in that it is a sort of fictitious historical period. The names of my characters have a strong connection with Dickens. Miss Slighcarp and Mr. Gripe, for example—this is the kind of name Dickens uses a great deal. A lot of my names, in fact, I tend to think of in dreams. I just leave the business to my subconscious, and it produces some fine names.

It may sound rather pretentious, but after all, it is a fairly classic tradition to intersperse adventure with humor. In Shakespeare, for instance, this is quite a common feature.

As well as Dickens, I imbibed between the ages of seven and twelve a lot of the historical novels of Walter Scott. *Ivanhoe* and *The Talisman*, particularly, had a terrific effect on me. Poe's *Tales of Mystery and Imagination*, which I read to myself when I was about eight, influenced me very much indeed. I also read a good deal of poetry at this time. For instance, traces of *Kubla Khan* come out in several of my books, particularly in *The Whispering Mountain*.

When I was small, I absolutely loved *Little Women, Wide Wide World, Anne of Green Gables, Rebecca of Sunnybrook Farm,* and dozens of others, many of which seem to be about children who went to stay with hardhearted relatives on farms. I thought I'd like to produce the hardhearted relatives to end all, and that was the idea for *Nightbirds on Nantucket.* I'd always rather wanted to do a book with a New England setting, and Nantucket seemed the absolute quintessence of New England. Everybody on Cape Cod told me what a marvelous place Nantucket was, and I wanted to do a book about whaling because of this need to have the Atlantic crossed in a ship. So Nantucket seemed the obvious choice for a setting. I went to New Bedford first because my ancestors came from there. I looked at the Whaling Museum and then I went on to Nantucket.

> *All of Joan Aiken's books read aloud well. The stories move briskly along, with plots and subplots unfolding and then converging in a breathless finish. Starchy Victorian dialogue and rich descriptive words roll smoothly off the tongue.*

The first two chapters of *Willoughby Chase* were written when both my children were tiny, and then the book had to be put aside for almost ten years. By this time the children were much bigger, and I read the chapters aloud to them as I wrote. They made a lot of very useful comments and criticisms as we went along. I used to read aloud an enormous amount to my children, other books as well as mine, and some of them I found rather boring. It seemed to me it should be possible to write books which a grown-up, as well as a child, would find entertaining. Because of this, I write with the reader-aloud partially in mind. In *The Whispering Mountain,* I think possibly I slightly overdid all the vocabulary because I got hold of an absolutely marvelous book called *The Elizabethan Underworld* by A. B. Judges. It gave page after page of the most super Elizabethan slang which seemed so beautiful to me I couldn't resist putting in great chunks of it. I have heard that children enjoy these words very much. But combined as they are with a good deal of Welsh and a bit of Scotch which somehow found its way in, I can see it's rather difficult for the adult reader-aloud.

It's terribly hard to say how I work out my plots. They seem to gradually accrue. But what I try to do is start off with some crisis or problem situation, such as in *Willoughby Chase*, where the children are left in charge of these villains. In *Black Hearts in Battersea*, the boy comes up to London expecting to stay with his friend and finds the friend unaccountably vanished. The hero in *The Whispering Mountain* is rejected by his grandfather, and the grandfather in turn is being rejected by the townspeople, so that right away there is some problem. I do, in fact, work out the plot entirely before I start to write, but then often it changes as I go along.

When I planned *Willoughby Chase* I hadn't thought at all of following it up with the other books. But when I finished it, I'd enjoyed it so much and my publisher seemed to enjoy it, that it seemed the natural thing to go on and write a sequel. The fourth, *The Whispering Mountain*, is in the same period but not connected as yet. Now I am going to go on and do a fifth in which all the characters are going to meet in some way which I haven't resolved.

It was the most tremendous fun writing those books. You know, I wrote them very largely to please myself.

My father didn't actually influence me to begin writing, but he was very pleased when I did and gave me a lot of encouragement. Nearly all of my family write. I have a sister who writes historical novels, and my elder brother has suddenly broken into the field. He is really a scientist, but he has written a novel about industrial espionage and a science fiction novel. I believe my younger brother is in the middle of a novel. No doubt my children will take to it, too.

Joan Aiken herself has been writing since she was five, when she spent her month's pocket money on a large blue notepad and began to fill it with stories and poems. "Writing," she says, "is just the family trade."

Some Books by

JOAN AIKEN

ARABEL'S RAVEN. Illus. by Quentin Blake. New York: Doubleday, 1974. 118p.

> When Arabel's father brings home an injured raven, the Jones family has no inkling of the adventures in which Mortimer will involve them. In three stories, Joan Aiken tells the improbable tales of Mortimer's encounters with robbers, a hospital, and a babysitter.

BLACK HEARTS IN BATTERSEA. Illus. by Robin Jacques. New York: Doubleday, 1964. 240p.

> Simon arrives in London to study art, only to discover that Dr. Field, who was to sponsor him, has disappeared. With his old friend Sophie from Gloober's Poor Farm and his new friend Dido Twite, he takes part in a wild series of misadventures in which a scheme to kill the king is thwarted and the rightful heir to the old Duke of Battersea is found.

THE CUCKOO TREE. Illus. by Susan Obrant. New York: Doubleday, 1971. 314p.

> Dido Twite has returned to England from her adventures aboard a whaler in *Nightbirds on Nantucket*. With her is Captain Hughes who has a secret dispatch destined for the Admiralty. On the way to London to deliver the dispatch, their coach overturns and Captain Hughes is injured. They are forced to accept the grudging hospitality of queer Lady Tegleaze and frightening Mrs. Lubbage. There follows a series of adventures, in which a missing heir is found and a plot to roll St. Paul's Cathedral into the Thames is foiled. The imperturbable Dido brings her friends through it all and sees to it that the dispatch is delivered, good King Richard is crowned, and St. Paul's is saved.

THE KINGDOM AND THE CAVE. Illus. by Victor Ambrus. New York: Doubleday, 1960. 160p.

> A new illustrated edition of a story written by Joan Aiken when she was seventeen.
>
> Prince Michael and his cat Mickle are the prime movers in a plan to prevent the Down Under people from invading the upper world. Basic animal language for Michael, a wishing collar for Mickle, and

other magical appurtenances make it possible for Michael and assorted animal helpers to save the kingdom.

MIDNIGHT IS A PLACE. New York: Viking, 1974. 287p.

The grim city of Blastburn, a pair of indomitable children, and Joan Aiken's intricate plotting are all here again, but the result is a more serious novel than the tongue-in-cheek melodrama of *Willoughby Chase* and its sister stories. Lucas and Anna-Marie have, for different reasons, become the wards of Sir Randolph Grimsby, splenetic owner of the huge carpet factory known as Midnight Mill. When Sir Randolph is killed in the fire which destroys Midnight Court, the children are thrown on their own in the streets of Blastburn. In all the extraordinary events that fate has in store for them, they rise to the occasion and prove their mettle. Through it all run the themes of the intolerable conditions for children working in nineteenth-century mills and the debasement of the human being who lives always in poverty.

THE MOONCUSSER'S DAUGHTER; a play for children. Illus. by Arvis Stewart. New York: Viking, 1973. 95p.

Saul, the lighthouse keeper who has formerly been a wrecker, keeps visitors as well as his daughter away from the lighthouse. By keeping them away, Saul keeps secret the green monster Caliban and his treasured book, both of them hidden below the lighthouse in an old shipwreck. Many try to steal the treasure, but the keeper's daughter manages to foil them all.

NIGHTBIRDS ON NANTUCKET. Illus. by Robin Jacques. New York: Doubleday, 1966. 216p. o.p.; Dell, paper.

Dido, after the wreck which comes near the end of *Black Hearts in Battersea*, is picked up by an American whaling ship whose eccentric captain is chasing the pink whale. Dido and the captain's daughter, Dutiful Penitence, are left on a Nantucket farm to be cared for by Aunt Tribulation. The girls soon find that Tribulation is not all that an aunt should be and that the Battersea intrigue has reached as far as Nantucket. Old enemies reappear, but new friends and the captain's elusive pink whale help to vanquish them.

NIGHTFALL. New York: Holt, 1969. 128p.

When nine-year-old Meg's mother and stepfather are killed in an automobile crash, she returns to London to live with a father she hardly remembers. Her lonely life in her father's austere household is lightened by the friendship of Polly and her brother George, to whom Meg becomes engaged at eighteen. The increasing terror of a recurring nightmare impels her to get at its cause before her marriage. When she learns that she had been the victim of a childhood accident that had been followed by amnesia, she returns to the scene of the accident. As memory begins to waken, she finds her life in danger again.

NOT WHAT YOU EXPECTED. New York: Doubleday, 1974. 320p.
Humor and tragedy distinguish this collection of fanciful short stories selected from three of the author's books originally published in England. The plots and subjects are varied and original, ranging from ghosts to dragons to doll-size humans.

THE WHISPERING MOUNTAIN. Illus. by Frank Bozzo. New York: Doubleday, 1968. 237p.
Living in the little Welsh town of Pennygaff with his grandfather, curator of the museum, Owen is implicated when the legendary Golden Harp is stolen. In his pursuit of the missing harp, Owen is aided and abetted by his friend Arabis, as well as the Seljuk of Rum, and the little people who live under the mountains.

WINTERTHING; a play for children. Illus. by Arvis Stewart. New York: Holt, 1972. 79p.
Four children and their mad aunt come to live on a small, cold island off Scotland. In the course of making it livable they learn much about their own characters, but more about the power of the Winterthing which holds the island in thrall every seventh year. And too late for some of them, the children learn the secret of their own past.

THE WOLVES OF WILLOUGHBY CHASE. Illus. by Pat Marriott. New York: Doubleday, 1963. 168p.
When Bonnie's parents leave for a long sea voyage, Miss Slighcarp comes to the isolated mansion at Willoughby Chase to act as governess for Bonnie and her cousin Sylvia. Miss Slighcarp and Mr. Grimshaw, her accomplice in villainy, appropriate the estate and hustle Bonnie and Sylvia to Blastburn to Mrs. Brisket's dreadful home for orphans. Goose boy Simon helps them escape and the three companions make their way to London. With good Lawyer Gripe's assistance, the plot is foiled and justice triumphs.

Victor G. Ambrus

Born in Budapest, Hungary in 1935, Victor Ambrus was supposed to follow his father's career as a chemical engineer. But his leaning was toward drawing, and after completing grammar school he was accepted at the Hungarian Academy of Fine Art. He later made his way to England, where he has lived since that time.

In England he entered the Royal College of Art. He began his book career even before graduation, when a publisher commissioned him to illustrate a book. It was not until he had illustrated a number of books for other authors that he tried writing and illustrating his own. His first effort was *The Three Poor Tailors*, and it was awarded the Kate Greenaway Medal.

Mr. Ambrus's great interest is old weapons and historical battles. He collects antique weapons, mostly swords from the Napoleonic period, as well as old engravings of battles. He particularly likes to draw battle scenes and has taken up fencing and horseback riding to give his drawings authenticity. Inspired by his collection of arms and armor, he has begun to write books for older children on military history.

Mr. Ambrus and his wife met while they were both students at the Royal College. They live now in Surrey with their son Mark. Since Mrs. Ambrus collects dolls and Mark has a fossil collection, a favorite family activity is hunting down more items for their collections.

Interview

Victor Ambrus has illustrated books for older boys and girls and has written and illustrated picture books for young children. How did he become interested in illustrating children's books?

I suppose it really started right at the beginning, when I started reading books. As soon as I read a story, I was immediately inspired to do a drawing. I was also very interested in the books I saw that were illustrated by other artists, and I tried to imitate their drawings. When I went to school (to grammar school) afterwards, I didn't do an awful lot of drawing; but when I entered an art school, I immediately took up illustrating again, together with the other subjects I learned.

I think I work in the colors that I use because they appeal to me more than anything else. I hope they also appeal to children, but I enjoy using brilliant colors enormously because I find them exciting to use. I like to use clear colors, anyway, because I think if you mix colors—with big blacks and whites, for instance—you get a lot of gray. I don't particularly like to use color the way painters would use it, mixing it up too much. I like to put the colors straight down, whether it's ink or poster paint. Also, I feel that folktales are a form of folk art, like embroidery or painting on wooden furniture, and they are always done with brilliant colors. It's only natural that books should also be illustrated in bright colors.

I suppose other artists must have influenced my work. I am very interested in Victorian illustrators' work, particularly Arthur Rackham's books. I have enormous admiration for them. So probably the way they work appeals to me, and I like to be influenced by them.

Naturally, Hungary has influenced my work more than anything else. I spent much of my childhood in the countryside, although I lived in the city. During the summer holidays we used to go down to the country and I had some marvelous times there, especially in the Hungarian villages around us. They were a tremendous influence on my work. But every time I visit different countries, I feel like doing picture books on different subjects.

I'd like to do something with Indians. When I went to Canada, I met some Indians and I thought they were fascinating characters. I would very much like to do a story on them.

Mr. Ambrus has retold and illustrated several Hungarian folktales.

I got a little book that my mother sent out to me, a curious little book called *List of Recordings of Folk Tales*, as told by old peasants and old ladies in the villages in Hungary. Very often these people are very outspoken, and some of the tales are quite rude, really, but they've got this original flavor about them which makes them very easy to read. I read through a great many of them until I find one which I can visualize in terms of pictures. That's how I came to start on the picture books I've done so far. But I hope to find a lot of different subjects in addition to the Hungarian folktales that I've done.

It is always a difficult problem to illustrate books by other authors, because you've got to try and work out what is in the mind of an author, what type of character he has in mind. But generally speaking, the better the book, the easier to illustrate. If I read a very good description of a character, then I immediately get an idea of the character without any difficulty. Often I get books where the characters are vaguely described and the reader does not get an immediate and definite idea of what they would look like and how they would behave. Then I am in great trouble illustrating the different characters. I firmly believe if you get a good story you get good illustrations, and if you get a mediocre story or a bad story you can end up with bad drawings. The artist doesn't have much of an idea of what the character is really like. Therefore, the artist is guessing, and he will probably draw very average characters rather than a real believable person. I have talked to authors about the illustrations I have done for their books. Quite often we found that the image of the character I had in mind is the same type of character that they wrote about in the book. At the same time I had an author who said my illustrations influenced her writing. It was Mrs. Peyton. She said that she was surprised to see some of the drawings I did of characters, and then later on she thought perhaps that's the way they should be, and she molded that character in the next book to match the drawings in a way. I always feel very pleased if I hear that I managed to portray a character as the author pictured him.

Quite often I have to go to the location of the setting of a book before I do the illustrations. If I have the time, I try to. But, of course, when you get books on Africa it's a bit difficult. I have gone to the location of several of the books, which is very exciting. In fact, I've done some of the drawings on the spot, and they always seem to have much more of a feeling of reality about them. I remember once drawing in a town in the bitter cold when my hands were absolutely numb—I could just about hold a pen—but those drawings have a feeling of reality about them which is lacking in the drawings I did in the comfort of my house. So it's always a good thing to go to the location of a place and get the feeling of that place.

Generally speaking, I choose which events I illustrate in a story. Very occasionally, when there is a small amount of space available in the book, you get restricted by the publisher. The editor determines exactly the places where drawings are needed, and you have to illustrate the text exactly, on the opposite side. I learned the hard way that the illustrator should always choose his subject. I remember that the second or third book I illustrated was a folktale which had a character in it, a girl with a spotted dress. There were twelve illustrations in the book—twelve full-page illustrations— and on every single page there was this girl in the spotted dress. Of course, the whole book became rather boring because every time you turned a page and you saw a drawing, there was this poor thing sitting in a spotted dress. The other thing was that out of the dozen drawings, she was sitting down in probably half of them. She was either sitting down in the kitchen or sitting down outside. Certainly the drawings became rather boring. I certainly was very bored with them. So if I can, I always ask the publishers to let me choose the incidents to illustrate.

There are two ways of deciding how many illustrations might be in a book. First, it depends on the amount of space available in the book after the type is placed. You're always given a guideline by the publisher of roughly how many pages can be spared for illustration. Other than that, the number of illustrations is the artist's own decision and depends upon the individual book. Some books dealing with sea stories or large-scale battles need double-spread illustrations that run across two pages. Obviously when you are doing an illustration that runs across two pages, there's not going to be very much space left for other illustrations, so the illustrations tend to be rather large-scale and few in number. But when you have a book with several small chapters, then you really need to do roughly a drawing each. So you are going to end up with a lot of small illustrations, probably chapter-head size or even smaller. I think the important thing is that the illustrations should be spaced out evenly through the book, so you don't have dull passages where there isn't any drawing at all.

I think that probably the most important thing to me in illustrating a book is to liven up the story and help it along. I think the illustration shouldn't just be a support of the text, but should take it a stage further. The illustration of a story should be very much a part of the book itself. It should also tell its own story. For instance, I once illustrated a book set in the period of the Battle of Trafalgar. I included in my illustrations some drawings of an incident on board Lord Nelson's battleship the *Victory*, which the author didn't deal with specifically, just mentioned on the side. When I had done the illustrations, she questioned my right to include drawings which didn't exactly tally with the text that she wrote. I explained to her I felt that at that particular part, the drawing was essential to bring out the atmosphere of the battle and the tragedy of what was happening, and in some way I felt that I was obliged to contribute to her story and take it along a stage further.

I know that when I was a young boy, I always used to be very influenced by the illustrations in a book. In fact, I remember picking up books in the library and looking at the illustrations, deciding whether to read a book or not on the basis of the drawings. I hope that by doing better illustrations, I encourage children to pick up books and read them.

The innkeeper called the guards

One of the illustrations that appears in color in *The Three Poor Tailors* (Harcourt, Brace), a Hungarian folktale retold, and illustrated, by Victor G. Ambrus.

who chased them through the town.

Some Books by

VICTOR AMBRUS

BRAVE SOLDIER JANOSH. New York: Harcourt, 1967. unp.
Janosh is an old soldier who has spent most of his life away from his Hungarian village. The villagers listen raptly to his stories, especially the one he tells here of his encounter with Napoleon and his army. Janosh, of course, defeats Napoleon's army singlehandedly and becomes the great Napoleon's friend.

A COUNTRY WEDDING. Reading: Addison-Wesley, 1975. unp.
A fox and a wolf, learning of a wedding, steal some trousers and arrive at the party uninvited to enjoy the feast. When they are caught and punished, they decide that in the future they will forego all wedding feasts.
As in all Mr. Ambrus's picture books, the simple plot is enhanced by gay and charming illustrations.

THE LITTLE COCKEREL. New York: Harcourt, 1968. unp. o.p.
Scratching in the rubbish heap one day, the old woman's cockerel finds a gold coin to give to his mistress. But the Sultan demands the coin for himself. When the cockerel tries to get the coin back, the Sultan has him thrown into the well, then into the fire, and finally into the beehive. Each time the cockerel escapes, until at last the Sultan gives back the coin. The brave little cockerel goes home to his mistress and never has to scratch in the rubbish heap again.

THE SEVEN SKINNY GOATS. New York: Harcourt, 1969. unp.
Jano plays his flute so well that everyone wants to dance to it. First the innkeeper's goats dance until they are skinny. Then the innkeeper himself cannot stop dancing. When the townsfolk exhaust themselves dancing, Jano is ordered out of town. Never again, he says, will he go to a town where people don't appreciate good music.

THE SULTAN'S BATH. New York: Harcourt, 1971. unp.
It is a very dry country and all the water must be used for the Sultan's bath. When the Sultan's bath water begins to disappear, Gul-Baba's secret garden is discovered. But the gardener discovers a way to have a bath for the Sultan *and* a garden.

THE THREE POOR TAILORS. New York: Harcourt, 1965. unp.

After celebrating at the inn, the three poor tailors have no money to pay the bill. When they try to run away without paying, they learn that their nanny goat is not quite fast enough to escape the town guards. Now they are working very hard to buy a billy goat.

Awarded the Kate Greenaway Medal, 1965.

Edward Ardizzone. Photograph courtesy of Oxford University Press.

Edward Ardizzone

*E*dward Ardizzone was born in Haiphong, Indochina (Vietnam) in 1900 and was sent to school in England when he was five years old. Although he spent his childhood in the small coastal town of Ipswich, where he learned a lot about the sea, he believes he inherited his real love of the sea from his paternal grandfather and maternal great-grandfather, both sea captains. His great-grandfather was also a fine amateur artist who kept a beautifully illustrated log of all his voyages.

Mr. Ardizzone and his three brothers and two sisters had the usual pattern of education for the English middle classes, with a series of governesses and then private and public school.

By 1929, although he had very little money, he was living the life of a professional artist. He had illustrated his first book and had had a small exhibition of his watercolors.

He joined the Territorial Army in 1939, and for seven months he was Gunner, Bombardier, Sergeant, and Lieutenant. Then, because he had had such a wide range of experience, he was appointed Official War Artist in the North African and European theaters of war. This was a most acceptable assignment because he was doing exactly what he wanted to do—paint.

Mr. Ardizzone has received many honors over the years. One of the most important was the Kate Greenaway Medal awarded in 1956 by the Library Association of Great Britain for his picture book *Tim All Alone*.

In addition to his own books, he has illustrated many books written by other authors. Two of those he especially enjoyed illustrating are *Peacock Pie* by Walter de la Mare and the Faber edition of *Pilgrim's Progress* by Paul Bunyan.

Mr. Ardizzone is a warm and friendly man who enjoys having children around him. He and his wife now live in County Kent in pretty orchard country about 50 miles from London.

Mr. Ardizzone has written a book about his childhood, youth, and young manhood, *The Young Ardizzone: An Autobiographical Fragment* (New York: Macmillan, 1971. 144p.). The book covers the period up to 1936, when *Little Tim and the Brave Sea Captain* was published, and is profusely illustrated with Mr. Ardizzone's black-and-white and color wash illustrations.

Interview

Well, I suppose in a way Little Tim's adventures came from my childhood imaginings, because I've always loved the sea but I never wanted to run away to sea. Tim's adventures had a bit of truth in them because when I was a little boy I lived in a town called Ipswich. Now, Ipswich is a seaport. Little ships come up there—little coastal ships, the sailing barges, the small steamboats— and I used to play on the docks. I used to go aboard the ships. I had a marvelous time. I got chased off sometimes, of course. The only sea voyage I had as a little boy was when I came all the way from China to England.

My sisters and I had a curious childhood because my father worked in the Far East and we were more or less like Kipling's children. We were farmed out to people. I mean, I didn't see my mother for three or four years at a time when I was a little boy, and there were dreadful moments. I'll never forget one birthday time going to the school notice board, and finding not a thing on it—not a letter or a notice for a package. Now that's a traumatic experience for a little boy. It was understandable that my gifts and letters might be a few days late coming from China, but to a small boy, there is no reason for such a disappointment.

Well, I suppose I was my own teacher. You see, I had a very curious start. About 1918 I was eighteen years old and had to get a job. My parents weren't going to keep me, so I got a job as a statistical clerk in the city of London. I had always wanted to paint and draw, but I had no idea of being a professional artist. That job was a very strange one. It was adding up figures all day, and I got very quick at adding. So, instead of being what I call a good apprentice, asking for more work, I used to do nothing but doodle, nothing but doodle. In the evenings, four nights a week, I used to go to classes, learning to draw only. Then my father gave me some money. I threw up my job, and the poor old man nearly had a stroke. "That nice safe job! My boy, what are you doing?" Anyhow, he gave me money which kept me going for a short time. I went to an art school for one day, and they gave me a still life to paint. It bored me so much that I never darkened the doors of an art school again.

In 1936 I published my first book. The writing came quite by chance, by telling the story of *Little Tim and the Brave Sea Captain* to my son Phillip and my daughter Christina, the young woman you saw here. They were little then, and they liked it. Little Tim was really my son Phillip, a little boy just like Tim with his pale hair. To tell you the truth, I was very broke at the time. All young artists are terribly broke at moments, and I thought I would try to sell the story. I wrote it in a great big sketch book. I did the drawings and I wrote the text in by hand. I tried it 'round the publishers, but no publisher in England would take it. Then a great friend of mine knew the head of the New York branch of the Oxford University Press. He liked it, took it over to America, and published it there.

Mr. Ardizzone has received national recognition as a painter as well as an author and illustrator of children's books.

I'm a painter first. I paint pictures. You see, I started out in life to be a painter, and I've always kept it up because I think it's very important that illustrators should paint pictures first and then do more illustrations. The paintings are a refreshing thing that help you with the illustrations. Otherwise, you pour out the same little formula all the time, and that's very dangerous.

Mr. Ardizzone discusses how he molds the story and the illustrations together.

I start with an idea. I don't write the story first. The story and illustrations go hand in hand. Very often, I'll write a bit and then I'll do a drawing. Then I'll realize I won't have to do nearly so much writing because the drawing tells the story. And I use the balloons for a very definite reason. The point is, you see, that if you have a balloon with a little bit of speech in it, it is equivalent to half a page of text. For instance, you have Mr. Blogs saying, "I can't, it hurts 'orrible." And the mate says, "Mutiny, Mr. Blogs." That describes the whole situation, which would take a whole page to describe in writing.

Most of my stories come from stories I've told to children, then they have to be tidied up a bit. I've got favorites besides the Little Tim stories. I'm very, very fond of *Paul, Hero of the Fire*. And I like the one called *Diana and the Rhinoceros* because that's really for my daughter's children. That's the house they live in, in Richmond. That's a story I told to them off-the-cuff one afternoon when we were staying in a little place in the south of France. And *Johnny the Clockmaker*. Yes, I like that, too. Now that was my son Nick's story. We were living in Wales then. It was during World War II. I had just come back on leave from the Middle East. I remember telling him that one afternoon.

The reactions of the children in Mr. Ardizzone's books are so childlike. We asked him how he accomplishes this.

Well, I suppose I haven't grown up myself. I can't see any other way. I just write as I can. And I enjoy myself doing it.

Mr. Ardizzone comments on the pleasures of reading his books aloud to children.

It's funny, you know, when you read aloud to children. Some think you're marvelous, and others are bored. You can't tell. I really think a reader is much better. I've heard my stories read aloud by an actor, most beautifully done, and the voice was so good. The way it was read was marvelous. It held their attention. The author is really the worst reader in some ways.

Mr. Ardizzone comments on his illustrating of books by other authors.

When a publisher asks me to illustrate a book by another author, he tells me the number of pages the illustrations must amount to. So, if he says he wants twenty pages free for illustrations, then I know I can do forty half pages, or some quarter pages, some half pages, and some full pages. I see a book and I go through it saying, "I ought to have illustrations scattered throughout the book." An illustrator should be able to illustrate any part of a book he wishes. I just read the text and decide what parts of the book I will illustrate and what kind of drawings I'm going to do for it.

My aim when writing and illustrating children's books is really to amuse myself. I don't try to educate children. I don't consciously try to preach a moral. Morals come into it, they're bound to, but I don't consciously try to do any of those things. I just write a story that amuses me, and hope that it also amuses children.

Some Books by
EDWARD ARDIZZONE

DIANA AND THE RHINOCEROS. New York: Walck, 1964. 32p.
> One late winter afternoon Diana and her parents are having tea, when the door slowly opens and a huge rhinoceros comes in. Her mother screams, her father runs, but Diana knows about rhinoceri and she notices the animal has a very bad cold. She kindly leads it to the fireplace where it can rest, and gives it large doses of Influenza Mixture, Cough Cure, and two hundred aspirin, followed by piles of hot buttered toast. The rhinoceros feels better at once. Diana keeps the rhinoceros as a pet for the rest of her life, and whenever it has a cold she gives it large doses of medicine and piles of hot buttered toast.

JOHNNY THE CLOCKMAKER. New York: Walck, 1960. unp.
> Johnny likes to saw and hammer and put pieces of wood together to make things. He has a book that tells him how to make clocks, but when he decides to make a grandfather clock his parents scoff

A reproduction of the watercolor cover illustration executed by Edward Ardizzone for the 1955 edition of *Little Tim and the Brave Sea Captain* (Walck).

and his friends at school tease and bully him. Only Susannah and Joe, the blacksmith, believe that he can do it. With their help and encouragement Johnny makes a fine grandfather clock, and he goes on to be the finest clockmaker in the country.

LITTLE TIM AND THE BRAVE SEA CAPTAIN. New York: Walck, 1936. unp.
Mr. Ardizzone's *Little Tim* stories have delighted young children for years. In this first one, Tim runs away from home and goes to sea as a stowaway. When he is discovered, the angry captain orders that Tim be put to work scrubbing decks and helping in the galley. On the voyage, the ship runs into a violent storm and crashes on a rock. Tim and the captain are the last to be rescued. When the captain meets Tim's parents, he tells them what a brave sailor Tim is.

LUCY BROWN AND MR. GRIMES. New York. Walck, 1970. 48p.
Orphaned Lucy is a very lonely little girl who lives with her aunt. After Lucy meets lonely old Mr. Grimes he and his housekeeper often invite her to tea. Lucy and Mr. Grimes become fast friends, and when the doctor says Mr. Grimes must move to the country, he asks Lucy's aunt if Lucy might go along. They have a beautiful house and gardens, and Mr. Grimes buys Lucy a white pony. Lucy thinks it is the loveliest place she has ever seen.

NICHOLAS AND THE FAST-MOVING DIESEL. New York: Walck, 1959. 48p.
When the engineer and fireman of a steam train fall ill from poisoned tea, Nicholas and Peter save the train from a disastrous accident. As a reward, they are each given a large sum of money and lessons on how to drive a diesel engine. Soon they are driving the fastest train in England—the Midland Flyer.

PAUL, THE HERO OF THE FIRE. New York: Walck, 1962. unp.
Paul decides that he has to earn some money so his father won't have to sell their house. He gets a job at the Giant Circus turning the children's merry-go-round. Even though the work is hard, Paul likes it there. He makes new friends, and every day is filled with excitement. But nothing is so exciting as the day of the fire, when he leads the children to safety and saves the horses and the lions. All the people who work at the Giant Circus think Paul is very brave, and the manager gives him a fine reward that helps his father very much.

PETER THE WANDERER. New York: Walck, 1964. unp.
The old sailor tells Peter he has been wandering the world in search of a treasure locked in a chest that can be opened only by the gold

key he wears on a chain around his neck. Soon after the old man has gone, Peter finds the key lying in the road. He must find the old man and return the key to him. Peter's search is difficult and he has many adventures. He uses all his wit and daring to survive the dangers of the long journey.

SARAH AND SIMON AND NO RED PAINT. New York: Delacorte, 1965. 48p.
Sarah and Simon are children of a talented artist. He paints beautiful pictures, but few people buy them, and so they are very poor. Their father needs more red paint to finish his masterpiece, which someone has offered to buy. While trying to find a way to get the paint, Sarah and Simon unknowingly bring good fortune to the family.

TIM ALL ALONE. New York: Walck, 1956. unp.
Tim has been away on a long holiday, and when he returns to his home by the sea, the house is boarded up and his mother and father are gone. He is very sad, for he longs to see them. There is nothing he can do but go in search of them. It is a long journey, and Tim endures many hardships before he is reunited with his parents.
Awarded the first Kate Greenaway Medal in 1956.

TIM'S LAST VOYAGE. New York: Walck, 1972. unp.
Tim and Ginger sign up as deckhands for a three-day voyage on the *Arabella*. They are warned that the bosun is a tartar. True to his reputation, he bullies and overworks the boys. When the ship is lost in a violent storm, the captain is worried, the crew is frightened, and the cowardly bosun flees to his cabin. It is Tim who remains calm in the midst of disaster. After the crew is rescued and Tim returns home, he promises his mother he will never go to sea again until he is grown.

WRONG SIDE OF THE BED. New York: Doubleday, 1970. unp.
A story without words tells of a little boy's day on which everything he does seems to be wrong. He must have gotten out of bed on the wrong side.

THE LITTLE GIRL AND THE TINY DOLL. By Edward and Aingelda Ardizzone. New York: Delacorte, 1966. unp.
While her mother is shopping in a grocery one day, a little girl sees a tiny doll out of reach among the frozen food boxes in a deepfreeze bin. The doll is frightened and cold, and as the boxes are moved

around she is almost crushed. Several times the little girl takes warm clothes to the tiny doll, and when she is permitted to take the doll home, their brief relationship grows into a lasting friendship.

Other books in the Little Tim series are:

TIM AND CHARLOTTE. New York: Walck, 1951, unp. o.p.

TIM AND GINGER. New York: Walck, 1965. unp.

TIM AND LUCY GO TO SEA. New York: Walck, 1958. unp.

TIM IN DANGER. New York: Walck, 1953. unp.

TIM TO THE LIGHTHOUSE. New York: Walck, 1968. unp.

TIM TO THE RESCUE. New York: Walck, 1949. unp.

TIM'S FRIEND TOWSER. New York: Walck, 1962. unp.

Ruth Arthur. Photo courtesy of Atheneum Publishers.

Ruth Arthur

Ruth Arthur began her writing career at eighteen, when several of her short stories were published. At that time, and later when her own children were small, she wrote stories for young children. When the youngest of her six children reached her teens, Miss Arthur started to write stories for older girls. She actually began writing, however, when she was much younger. She was a great reader, and English was her favorite school subject. Each week there was an assigned essay to write, and she and her good friend competed with each other for the best essay.

Her childhood was spent in Scotland. Her mother died when Miss Arthur was only two weeks old, and for a time she lived with relatives. When her father remarried, she moved with her father and stepmother to the country, and the family eventually grew to six children.

At eighteen, Miss Arthur went to London to take a teacher-training course. It was here that her first children's stories were published and she told some of her own stories on radio programs.

Her four daughters and two sons are grown now, and Miss Arthur and her husband live in Swanage on the south coast of England. She comes to the United States occasionally to visit a son and daughter and enjoys the opportunity while here to talk with American young people about her books.

Interview

I've written since I was about six years old, I think. I used to write poetry when I was a little girl. When I was ten years old, we had a competition at school to write a war poem. This was the First World War. I wrote a war poem and I got the prize for the under-twelves. When I got home (I was at boarding school) my father said, "What is this I hear that you have a prize for poetry? You can't write poetry." "I can," I replied, "I suppose I can. I wrote it." And I produced the poem. I'd used a lot of very difficult words. I hadn't always gotten the meaning quite right, but they must have been words which I'd heard and put in, you see. "You couldn't have written this by yourself," my father said, "You must have been helped. Someone your age wouldn't write a poem like this with these words in it." I said, "I can't help it. I did write it myself." I had a beautiful edition of the *Arabian Nights*, which I've still got, for my first prize. I think from then I just went on writing.

I was a child who liked to read a great deal. There was a room at the top of our house where I used to go to do my homework. We called it the playroom, but the younger children (I was the eldest in the family) didn't come up very much, and I used to go up to do my homework. When I finished my homework, I'd read up there and write up there. Nobody really knew very much about it for a long time. My grandfather, who wrote quite a bit himself and illustrated, not for publishing but for family things, was very interested. He died when I was fifteen. Then when I was eighteen, I had my first stories published. My father introduced me to a friend of his who was a publisher in Glasgow and they took three stories and put them into a book of collections. I was so terribly thrilled I couldn't believe it. I think they paid me a pound each for them or something like that, which was terrific wealth then. I won one or two newspaper competitions, just little things that encouraged one. But I didn't start writing teen-age books until my youngest daughter was a teen-ager. I started when she was about eleven or twelve. That was *Dragon Summer*.

I've always been very interested in the supernatural. I don't drag it in, but it seems to crop up of its own accord as the story unfolds. I think children enjoy this, too. They seem to rather appreciate a little bit of magic, if you could call it that.

There is a legend, I think, about Dido. But I wasn't really conscious of this, I wasn't really thinking of this, when I wrote *A Candle in Her Room*. I remember as quite a small child I read a book, and there was a bad doll in it who had a bad influence on this child. I have no idea what the book was. I don't know who it was written by. I remember it being read to me when I was quite small. It must have left some impression, because as soon as I started writing this story the bad doll just cropped up. She was there.

I think characters are very important and the plot certainly is. But, in a way, as your character develops, the plot can change a little bit. I think you have to be very much aware of the main structure of your plot before you start. But you can be taken by your characters into all kinds of sidelines and, of course, new characters keep coming in that you haven't really planned or expected.

I found Margarita (Meg) in *Portrait of Margarita* difficult to portray because I don't know West Indians very well, and, of course, she was partly West Indian. It was difficult to get the character authentic and not too English. I don't know whether I succeeded or not. I hope so.

A Candle in Her Room was turned down by one publisher because it was not thought that children would be at all interested in three different generations. Perhaps it's very difficult for an editor to judge this. I had had a good deal of experience with teen-agers and with my own children and their friends, and I think one pretty well knows what will go and what won't, what they like and what they don't. Why shouldn't they be interested in older people, especially if the older people start as children? They grow up and still in a way are children at heart. They don't change all that much.

It's a very old house in *A Candle in Her Room*, and I suppose I had the idea that different generations had grown up in it. As the story unfolded, the next generation and the next one came into it quite naturally. I didn't really start with the idea in my mind to have three generations, but it happened as the story grew. Which it does, of course. This is the exciting thing about writing. When you start a story and become involved in it, in a way it takes over, and all kinds of things which you never dreamt of writing about perhaps come into your story. This makes it very exciting, because it means that all the time you have to be reading about subjects you don't know enough about, finding out about things that perhaps are quite new to you. If you are going to mention any subjects such as adoption or anything like this, you have to read a tremendous amount and learn a great deal about it, so that you can write your little bit with authority.

The Saracen Lamp, too, is about a very old house with three completely different generations of children in it, three different periods of history. The first one very early, the thirteenth century, a girl; the next one, the time of Mary Tudor; and the last one completely up-to-date. It was a great one to write.

I have a particular age group in mind when I write, but I like to introduce grown-up problems at their own level to the eleven-, twelve-, thirteen-, fourteen-, and fifteen-year-olds. I think it is very difficult for them if they are reading grown-up books. They don't really get to the root of the trouble; it's all too impersonal. But if the problems happen to people of their own age, this is a much easier thing to understand. They begin to think about it, and this is a very important part of growing up.

I think relations between parents and children are a very serious problem. Each member of my own family, two sons and four daughters, has had difficulties with us. Although I think on the whole, at least I hope on the whole, we are fairly liberal parents. In my own childhood in Scotland, I was very strictly brought up, and there were a lot of things I had to fight about, and that I disagreed about, and was determined to get my way about. I am quite sure this will go on as long as there are children and parents.

A characteristic of Miss Arthur's books is that the setting seems to develop and sustain the mood of the story. Are the settings chosen with this in mind?

Not entirely. *Requiem for a Princess* came about because I had been ill and was listening to "Woman's Hour" on the radio and heard Ravel's *Pavane for a Dead Infanta*, and that just clicked something. That gave me the idea, and I thought about it for three years. The little Spanish princess was the original center of the idea, and I thought, "Well, I must get to Spain," so I planned a holiday there. About three weeks before I was going to the coast of Spain where there was a castle and all that was needed, the trip fell through because my friend couldn't go. It was too late to try and fix it with anyone else. I just cancelled it altogether and thought, "What a pity, I will have to keep it off for a bit." Then a friend wrote to me and said, "I'm going to Cornwall for a week, and it would be lovely if you could come, too." I thought, "Why not make the setting in Cornwall, the time of the Armada?" There were plenty of Spaniards who came over then in one way or another, so that's the reason I chose Cornwall for that. The house— I went down with a story in my mind and we travelled all around quite a lot. One day I saw a marvelous setting and a house that was old but not old enough, and I simply switched it and put a really old house in that place.

A Candle in Her Room takes place in Pembrokeshire in Wales, where we've had a holiday caravan for the children for eighteen years. We know the area very well and are very fond of it, and I just thought I would like to write a story about a family who lived in this beautiful countryside. I went out walking with my son one day, and I had the house very much in mind. Suddenly I saw it— absolutely right, exactly what I wanted. The story, I think, just grew as one wandered around and thought about it, and one knew the setting and the people and all this sort of thing so well. Of course, a lot of my own family came into it. My beloved old aunt was Liss. Liss was founded on her. The story just grew.

The Whistling Boy was set in Norfolk. I'd never been in Norfolk till about two years ago. A friend of mine bought a house there, and I went to stay with her. It's a very remote, wild part of the country—the seacoast, that is. One is tremendously conscious of the sea all the time. It's encroaching very much on the land, and there are these extraordinary salt marshes. There are great dunes dividing the sea from the land, with gaps in them here and there, and then a stretch of salt marsh inland. It's very flat country, and you feel at any time if there's a high tide or a great storm, the sea will break through and swamp the land, which it does repeatedly. There's one place in particular where there are two houses, and the sea has been coming in and coming in and chewing away at the cliff under these houses. When I first went there, one house had partially collapsed and the other house was left on the very brink of the cliff. Next time I went there that house was gone. They put up these huge breakwaters trying to stop the sea, but it gradually eats away. A lot of the old villages have been simply covered by the sea. The house in *The Whistling Boy* (it's a real house again) used to be twelve miles inland and now it's just a stone's throw from the sea. All this I found very fascinating and tremendously interesting. That's what started the idea of the story.

Illustrations are enormously important, but I think it matters very much who the illustrator is. I'm very lucky, indeed, because Margery Gill, who is a close friend of mine, does the drawings for my books. We're very much on the same wavelength. We look at things in the same way, and she takes enormous trouble to read my books very thoroughly, to take in any description that I've given. I try not to give too many descriptions, because I think the artist has to put her own personality into her drawings. If you restrict artists too much, you're not going to get the best from them. But she does read very carefully any descriptions that I make, and doesn't get them wrong. For example, if a girl is described with short hair, she doesn't give her long pigtails. Also, my houses and places are all real houses and real places. She always comes down and spends the day, and sees the place and makes sketches and takes great trouble over the setting. The setting is real and the people are not. They've got real characteristics, but they're all fictional. Therefore, she can make them up, as it were.

How did Miss Arthur manage to rear six children and find time to write books?

I jolly well made time—it wasn't easy! When the family was around, I had cooking and washing and ironing to do, and while I was doing these things I could think about my stories. Then the moment I had peace and quiet—waiting to pick somebody up from school in the car, going to London in the train, anywhere I could sit—I had my manuscript with me and would write even for a few minutes. If a thing is important enough to you, you make time for it.

Some Books by

RUTH ARTHUR

AFTER CANDLEMAS. Illus. by Margery Gill. New York: Atheneum, 1974. 121p.

Harriet, visiting a school friend on the Dorset coast, hears the story of young Ambrose Briddle who was drowned in 1890—after Candlemas. As Old Gramma Cobbley tells it, there is some question as to how he drowned, some connection with old pagan-like rites still celebrated at Candlemas. Harriet's curiosity about Ambrose fades somewhat when she finds a most unghostly boy hiding in one of the caves along the shore. Birney has run away from a boys' approved school (for those with criminal charges against them), and he is desperately in need of help and understanding. Harriet's efforts to win his trust are rewarded in the nearly tragic climax of the story.

THE AUTUMN PEOPLE. Illus. by Margery Gill. New York: Atheneum, 1973. 166p.

On her first visit to the island of Karasay, off the coast of Scotland, Romilly solves the mystery that had shadowed the life of her great-grandmother Millie. Millie's only visit to Karasay as a young girl had ended with the disappearance of Rodger Graham, her host's son, and she had refused afterward to visit the island again. Romilly's brief flights into her great-grandmother's time, where she is accepted as Millie by the ghosts of the past, lead her to discover the horrifying events which led to Rodger's disappearance.

A CANDLE IN HER ROOM. Illus. by Margery Gill. New York: Atheneum, 1966. 212p.

Melissa begins telling the story of herself and her sisters Briony and Judith. Briony finds the evil doll Dido in the old house where they live. But it is Judith, always the strange one of the sisters, who comes under the doll's corrupt spell. In the succeeding generations, Dido wields her diabolic influence with almost tragic results until her power is broken and the evil is exorcised.

DRAGON SUMMER. Illus. by Margery Gill. New York: Atheneum, 1962. 107p.

Kate spends a summer in a country cottage with her aunt and uncle and cousin Stephen. A dragon-shaped stone in the garden is the recipient of all kinds of gifts, including the key to a music box whose music brings a ghost to listen to its tune. Other things of a wonderful nature happen that summer. Merrity, mute for years, begins to speak, and Kate begins a lifelong friendship with a neighbor, Romilly. Years later, Kate returns to buy the cottage and make it her home. When lightning breaks open the dragon stone, she finds the music box key and sees her ghostly guest for the last time as he leaves the cottage in her hands.

THE LITTLE DARK THORN. Illus. by Margery Gill. New York: Atheneum, 1971. 195p.

Merrie cannot forgive her father for taking her from her Malayan mother and bringing her to live in Aunt Emma's house in England. Even his marriage to Birgit, whom she loves, does not bring them together. As she moves into her teens, the death of her little half-sister followed by her father's and Birgit's separation, seems to complete the break between them. But Birgit and her Norwegian family help her find direction and purpose in her own life and finally, understanding and forgiveness.

MY DAUGHTER, NICOLA. Illus. by Fermin Rocker. New York: Atheneum, 1965. 122p.

Nicola tries desperately to win the approval of her widowed father who, she feels, is disappointed that she is not a son. All her efforts to win his attention by her tomboy exploits fail, until her dangerous adventure in an abandoned mine leads her father to understand her desire for his approval.

PORTRAIT OF MARGARITA. Illus. by Margery Gill. New York: Atheneum, 1968. 185p.

When Meg's parents are killed in an airplane crash, Cousin Francis is named her guardian, and she lives in his home during school vacations. From her mother's West Indian family, Meg has inherited dark coloring, and in her new home and in school she finds enough prejudice to make her feel even more keenly the loss of her father's strength and love. The affection of Cousin Francis and some new friends bolster her self-confidence, and the love she finds on a trip to Italy helps her come to terms with her heritage.

REQUIEM FOR A PRINCESS. Illus. by Margery Gill. New York: Atheneum, 1967. 182p.

With the discovery that she was adopted, Willow becomes despondent and then ill. Sent to recover in an old house by the sea, she finds there a portrait of the Spanish girl Isabel, who had been the adopted daughter of the Tresilian family in the sixteenth century. Willow identifies herself with the portrait so completely that in her dreams she relives the story of Isabel. By involving herself in Isabel's problems, she solves her own, recognizing the strength of the love between her adopted parents and herself.

THE SARACEN LAMP. Illus. by Margery Gill. New York: Atheneum, 1970. 210p.

About 1300, Melisande marries Sir Hugh de Hervey. She leaves France to live in England at Littleperry Manor, which her young husband has built for her. She brings with her a jewelled golden lamp, the gift of her father's Saracen servant. The lamp brings strength and comfort in the joys and tragedies of her life. Two hundred years later, the lamp has become the treasure of the house. The story is now concerned with Alys, the Squire's unhappy illegitimate daughter. In the last segment, Perdita, a present-day descendant, is staying at Littleperry to recover from a crippling illness. She is haunted by the mystery of the Saracen lamp and senses the presence of the unhappy Alys. When another Saracen lamp comes into her hands, she is able to make the link between past and present and find her own place in the continuing history of Littleperry.

THE WHISTLING BOY. Illus. by Margery Gill. New York: Atheneum, 1969. 201p.

When her father remarries, Kirsty finds it impossible to accept her new young stepmother. Feeling that it might help to be away from her family for a while, Kirsty gets a job picking fruit in Norfolk for the summer holidays. There she meets Jake and learns about the ghostly Whistling Boy who almost led Jake to his death in the sea, an event Jake has blotted from his memory but which still fills him with unreasoning fear. In helping Jake and in understanding her friend Dinah, whom Kirsty feels she had failed earlier, Kirsty begins to grow up and sees her stepmother in a new light.

Nina Bawden. Photograph by Vivienne, London.

Nina Bawden

Nina Bawden has been writing since she was very young. Her first novel, still unpublished, was completed when she was eight years old. Of some of her other early writing Miss Bawden says: "I wrote plays for my toy theater and an epic poem in blank verse about a beautiful orphan with curly golden hair—my own was straight and dark."

She spent her childhood in suburban London. During World War II she and her brother were among the hundreds of children evacuated to safer areas of Great Britain. They spent some months in a small mining town in southern Wales, and then were sent to a farm in Shropshire. No doubt this is where she developed her desire to be a farmer, and for a while gave up her literary interests.

Her first book for children came about quite unexpectedly. She had always written adult novels, but when her children asked her to write a story about an exciting adventure they had had, she decided to try. It seemed to her that modern children's books lacked the vigorous and forceful quality of the Victorian novels which she had read and enjoyed as a child. She felt that writing for children must be the same as writing for adults. The books should present life honestly, with happiness and sadness, with excitement and discovery, but also with such negatives as poverty and loneliness. And so, she wrote, not with any age group in mind, but just to write an appealing story. Her children approved it, and she found that she enjoyed writing for children as much as, if not more than, writing for adults. Happily for her readers, she continues to write for children and to combine in her stories human understanding, adventure, humor, and suspense.

Miss Bawden and her husband, Austen Kark, who is in the European service of the British Broadcasting Corporation, live in Weybridge, Surrey. They have a teen-age daughter and two grown sons. Their interesting and attractive Victorian house has a garden and a large lawn in the back where they still play croquet when their children come to visit.

Interview

My younger son was eleven when I started writing for children, and he was very excited about my first book. He read it as it came out and made suggestions. I didn't always take his suggestions, but some of them I liked. Now our twelve-year-old daughter very much enjoys my books. With the last one, she brought in all her friends to hear it as it was written, chapter by chapter. They got very angry because I didn't produce the chapters as fast as they wanted them. I said there would be one a week, and I didn't always manage to do this. They got very cross and said that I should be more efficient.

I think there is a difference between the theme of a book, which is what the book is about, and the plot, which is the kind of mechanical part of how you make it work. I think I always know what the book is about before I start—that is, the theme. The plot does change a little bit as I go along.

Some of my books are real, of course. Some time ago there was an African boy in England whose father, a Prime Minister in Africa, was in prison. There was a great excitement for fear the boy would be kidnapped. I thought it would be very exciting if one had a chance like this to put the boy down in London and have some other children meet him and rescue him from a terrible political situation, a situation that was real enough and was also an adventure. And then they, too, would have an adventure with him. His two rescuers were also running away from something. The little girl, Lil, was running away from the welfare lady, because her mother was in the hospital and there was no one to look after her. The little boy was running away because his father was getting married again, and father and his bride didn't really want him around at that time. I think really most stories are adventure stories in a way, because most things that happen in life are adventures of one sort or another. It doesn't always have to be running away, and policemen, and fighting. It can be something much simpler, like the grandmother in *A Handful of Thieves* who had a wicked lodger who stole her savings. This is an adventure, too, and what happens to the children is an adventure. You can't have a story without suspense, can you, or you wouldn't want to go on reading?

When I'm choosing my characters, first of all, I think of somebody I would like to write about and people I would probably like, not just because they are good, or pretty, or clever, but because they are interesting. You think of a person, and you think what he looks like and how old he is, and the sort of things he is doing, and the sort of things that make him happy and unhappy, and the kinds of friends he's got, and the kind of family he's got, and the sort of places he lives in. And he grows up like that. Sometimes you use people you know or bits of people you know and put them together. Sometimes you make a person because you want that kind of person in your story. But sometimes you find that he develops on his own account, rather like the little girl, Lil, in *Three on the Run*. I thought I'd like a Cockney girl who wasn't educated, in order to set her against the African boy who was rather aristocratic and rich and well educated. I thought of Lil, who developed a very strong personality of her own. She didn't do it without me, of course, but she did seem to take over in a way that some characters do not. Sometimes the character is someone you've remembered. There is a book I wrote called *The White Horse Gang* that had a country boy called Abe in it. He was really a boy I knew during World War II when I lived on a farm. We thought it was wonderful because he could ride a horse, could shoot, and do all the things we couldn't do. He was a little bit older than we were. We admired him very much. I put him into this book really as he was, I think, a rather independent, wild boy. In the book he is very much as I remember Abe.

It is very difficult to know whether one has favorite characters or not. I think I like most of the children I write about. I wrote about Ben, who was in *The House of Secrets* as a little boy. I liked him so much that I thought he was far better than his brother and sister in the same book. He was a more mature person, and I thought it would be nice to write a book about him when he was a bit older. So he is the main character, really, in *Three on the Run*. I think he's grown up very well. I also like Lil in that book very much. I like Perdita in *The Witch's Daughter*, but then she was a rather unusual person because she'd been brought up so oddly. I like the little girl called Mary in *Runaway Summer*, too. She is a very bad-tempered, cross-grained, difficult, impossible child, but she is really quite nice underneath. In fact, she grows nicer as the book develops. I enjoyed writing about her because she was very cross, and when I was that age I was also very cross and wanted to hit people. So, I thought I would write about someone like that. Mary goes to live with her grandfather and Aunt Alice at the seaside because her parents are getting a divorce and she is very unhappy about it. She is lonely and has no one to play with, and because she is such a disagreeable little girl, it's not likely that she will find anyone. She has to leave her cat in London, too, and that only adds to her loneliness. She is down on the shore one day, and a boat lands with two men and a boy in it. The men run off and are picked up by the police. The little boy hides under a hut. He's an illegal immigrant, an Indian boy from East Africa. He's trying to get into England without a passport so that he can live with his uncle there. Mary rescues him. There is another child in the story, a policeman's son, who helps her hide the Indian boy on an island in an artificial grotto. The boy lives there all summer, until he becomes ill and they have to do something about it.

My choice of settings varies from book to book. *The Witch's Daughter* is different from all the others because that was a special setting in a sense. That story couldn't have happened anywhere else. We went on a holiday to the Isle of Mull which is off the coast of Scotland. We went with another family who had a little blind girl. We went climbing the mountains, exploring in the caves, walking along the very rocky shore, and rowing on the loch. It seemed that it would be a very lovely setting for a story, but I hadn't particularly thought of putting a book there. The oldest girl, whose name was Kate, said one day that it would be nice if I wrote a book about a blind girl because, she said, "Nobody puts blind children in books, except for sad, and it isn't fair."

So I said, "What sort of story would you like?" She said she'd like a story about Mull and about a blind girl who did something, something brave, like catching jewel thieves or robbers. Then other things happened when we were there. We went into a cave with the blind girl. Of course, it was quite dark in there and our torch battery went. We were very frightened because it was so dark. She wasn't frightened at all because she was blind and knew nothing but the dark. She didn't actually find the way out as the girl does in the story, but she said, "It's all right. We're here and if we go down to that spot," (she led us along) "you can call, and Dad will come with the lantern." And he did. That much of it was real, you see. I think that other settings for my books are really many places that I lived as a child or since I've been grown up. They are usually places that I've liked. I think I more often use settings that I like in children's books than in adult books. *The White Horse Gang* has its setting in Shropshire where I lived when I was small. *Three on the Run* is in London and in Herne Bay, a seaside town on the coast of Kent where my parents live. *A Handful of Thieves* is set—well, nowhere in particular—just in a town, but there is an old racetrack in the story, which is in fact near where I live now in Weybridge. It was very, very famous but isn't used any more.

Actually, I didn't deliberately set out to write for children. I was writing for grown-ups, and we were moving house. I'd finished a grown-ups' novel, and we were moving in three months' time. I thought I wouldn't have time to write another long adult novel. So my young son said, "Why don't you write a children's book?" I said I didn't think I could. My husband asked, "But it wouldn't take you as long as writing an adult book, would it?" I said that I didn't know, and he suggested that I try. So, I did, and it took me just as long as writing an adult book. But I enjoyed writing it so much that I thought that I would like to write some more. It's quite different—no, it's not different at all. It's just that I enjoy it more than writing adult novels.

And when boys and girls enjoy my books, it makes me want to write more. It's marvelous when they write and tell me they like my stories, and take the trouble to say what they like and why they like it. It's the most rewarding thing that can happen to a writer.

Some Books by

NINA BAWDEN

CARRIE'S WAR. Philadelphia: Lippincott, 1973. 159p.

When Hitler's bombs are falling so heavily on London, Carrie Willow and her little brother, Nick, are sent to a small Welsh mining town to live with dour Mr. Evans and his mousy younger sister. Life there is grim, until they meet Hepzibah Green who gives them love, good food, and a haven from the cruel discipline of Mr. Evans. But it is Hepzibah who tells them about the "screaming skull" and the curse that hangs over the house where she lives. Not until Carrie returns years later with her own children is she to know whether that curse has really been fulfilled.

A HANDFUL OF THIEVES. Philadelphia: Lippincott, 1967. 189p.

Fred McAlpine's grandmother is a friendly, independent little woman who doesn't want anyone to think that she can't take care of herself. When Gran misses her savings that she has been hiding in a teapot, Mr. Gribble, her "sinister lodger," is immediately suspected. Fred's friends, who all love Gran, decide to turn detectives and try to recover the money for her.

Miss Bawden has written a humorous, suspense-filled adventure story with many surprises.

THE HOUSE OF SECRETS. Illus. by Wendy Worth. Philadelphia: Lippincott, 1963. 190p.

It is an unhappy time for John, Mary, and Ben when they leave their father in Africa after their mother dies. They come to England to live with cross, scolding Aunt Mabel. They are lonely and sad, and yearn for their parents' love and understanding. But the children are fascinated by the large old house next door, with its high garden walls and its silent, deserted look. Ben's friendship with fey, old Miss Pin, and the secret passage the children find in Aunt Mabel's cellar wall, lead them to that house and right into serious trouble.

THE RUNAWAY SUMMER. Philadelphia: Lippincott, 1969. 185p.

When eleven-year-old Mary sees the small African boy abandoned on the beach by two strange-looking men, she forgets her own unhappy problems and, with the help of her friend Simon, decides to take care of the stranger. They take great risks and become entangled in deception and falsehoods in order to keep the boy hidden in a secret grotto on a deserted island. Throughout the summer they bring him food and care for him, until he becomes ill and they are forced to ask for help. Mary and Simon learn a lot about facing up to reality, and Mary discovers that life is not always unkind.

SQUIB. Philadelphia: Lippincott, 1971. 143p.

Squib isn't his real name. No one knows his real name, who his parents are, or where he lives. He is different—an odd, frightened, sad little boy who doesn't seem to belong to anyone. Somehow, Squib makes Kate think of her little brother Rupert. She has often wondered if Rupert really had been lost that summer four years ago, when, together, they had been swept by current and tide toward the open sea. Kate had been saved, but Rupert had never been found. He would be eight years old now, just about Squib's age. Could it be that Squib . . . ? In their search for Squib's identity, Kate, Robin, Prue, and Sammy encounter strange people and face real danger. There is the nasty woman in the tower, the uncouth boy at the Old People's Home, the grim mobile home site, and the quarry pit, where late one night, their adventures finally come to a terrifying climax.

THREE ON THE RUN. Philadelphia: Lippincott, 1964. 224p.

Adventure can come when you least expect it, and certainly Ben's adventure does. He has been visiting in London for a week, and now he is ready to go home. Bored and looking for something to do, he climbs the garden wall behind his father's flat, and unknowingly falls right into an international plot. There on the other side of the wall is Thomas, closely-guarded son of an exiled African leader then imprisoned in London. Ben, aided by his friend Lil, decides the only thing to do is to get Thomas out of London. Acting on a sudden impulse, they find a most unusual means of escape. A series of hair-raising events follow, all ending in an unexpected and thrilling climax.

THE WITCH'S DAUGHTER. Philadelphia: Lippincott, 1966. 181p.

Her name, Perdita, means the lonely one. People on the Scottish island of Shua where she lives think her mother has been bewitched. Children on the island are afraid of her. Her only companions are old Annie McLaren, her foster mother, and the mysterious Mr. Smith for whom Annie keeps house. During their summer vacation on the island, blind Jenny Hoggart and her brother Tim enjoy Perdita's friendship. Jenny, being blind, knows nothing of Perdita's odd clothes and her strangeness that makes other children stare. Before the summer is over, the three children are abandoned in a cave and are deeply involved in a police search for jewelry thieves.

The characters are carefully drawn and convincing. The suspense is skillfully maintained throughout the story.

THE WHITE HORSE GANG. Philadelphia: Lippincott, 1966. 188p.
Sam has long admired the rough and undisciplined Abe Tanner. Now that Sam's cousin Rose is coming to live with them, Sam fears that his new friendship with Abe might break up. Abe dislikes girls even more than Sam does, but Rose surprises them both. She isn't afraid when they tell her of the Gippet Wood and of some of the strange things that are happening there. Nor does she cringe when they tell her about the headless horseman. In fact it is Rose who molds the three into the White Horse Gang. They spend their days together, riding Abe's white mare, exploring the countryside, hatching up exploits that one day lead them to the brink of disaster.

Michael Bond

Michael Bond had his first success as a writer when a short story he wrote was accepted by *London Opinion*. It was 1945 and he was serving in the British Army in the Middle East. After this first publication, he continued to write short stories, articles, and radio plays. It was not until 1958 that he wrote his first book for children, *A Bear Called Paddington*.

Mr. Bond was born in Newbury and grew up in Reading. He was educated at Presentation College. After his Army service, he became a television cameraman with the British Broadcasting Corporation. He has since given that up in order to write full time.

He and his wife, whom he met at the BBC, live with their daughter in Haslemere in southern England. They lived in London before moving to the country, and Mr. Bond still does not consider himself a country person, though he counts gardening as one of his hobbies.

Living with the Bonds are the originals of his book characters: Thursday, a tiny plaster mouse; Harris, a small stuffed vole; Paddington, a worn tan bear puppet, and Paddington's satchel, a small, rather battered and scratched, brown suitcase. No doubt the real Olga da Polga lives with them, too.

Interview

> *Michael Bond is perhaps best known for his stories of the adventures of* A Bear Called Paddington. *Paddington is so real to his many fans that their very natural first question to Mr. Bond might be, "Is Paddington here?"*

He's upstairs.

The original Paddington was a very tiny bear I found in a London store one Christmas. He's really only about six inches tall. It sounds rather silly, but he'd been left on the shelf for Christmas all by himself. All the other bears had been sold, and I bought him as a present for my wife. In fact, I walked away and then I thought, "No, I can't leave him there," and I went back and bought him.

I didn't really intend to write the stories to be published. When I started writing stories about him, we were living near Paddington Station. I'd always wanted to use the name Paddington. That's how the first book was born. Then after a short while I had enough stories to fill a book. I called it *A Bear Called Paddington*. It went the rounds of the publishers. Eventually someone bought it and that was the start of the series.

Paddington has always seemed very real to me. I don't think you can really write a book unless you believe in the characters. To me Paddington is very, very real. If I walked down the Portobello Road and met him, I think we would both stop and have a chat, and I wouldn't be at all surprised.

I think a lot of Paddington's adventures are based on things that have happened to me. Very often if I have done something which, lucky for me, usually goes right, I think to myself, "What would happen if Paddington did it?" If I knock a hole in the wall, I think, "What would happen if Paddington knocked a hole in the wall?" This triggers off the idea. Most of the Paddington situations are really a case of thinking to myself, "What would happen if Paddington was doing this?" I thought of one story because I went to the dentist. As I was sitting in the dentist's chair, it suddenly occurred to me that Paddington had never been to the dentist, and I wondered what would happen if he went. Then I went to a horse show with my daughter and this triggered off another idea for a story because Paddington had never been horse riding, which I think might be difficult because of his short legs. I don't think he'd get them in the stirrups very easily.

One of my favorite stories, partly because it is my daughter's favorite, is where Paddington dines out in a big restaurant and gets in a terrible mess with pickled onions and throwing water over soufflés and things like this. I think my favorite Paddington story is always the next one I am going to write.

Each of the Paddington books is really seven distinct stories. I don't like starting a book until I have enough ideas to fill it, but Paddington is the sort of bear who is always getting into trouble. I keep a notebook, and when I have enough ideas for seven stories, I start the book. I probably keep a page of written notes for each chapter, just little headings for paragraphs and so on, and I start from there.

The publishers found Peggy Fortnum, who illustrates my Paddington books. In fact, when the first Paddington book came out, they did talk for some time of having photographs of a real bear in the zoo. As it turned out, it was a good thing they didn't. Then they thought of Peggy Fortnum, and she read the manuscript and liked it, which was a great thing. I think it shows in her drawings that she, too, is very fond of Paddington. We don't, in fact, meet very often. I write the books which get sent to the publisher, and they send a copy of the manuscript to Peggy Fortnum, and she gets on with the work. I often don't see the drawings until they come out in the book.

In a way I think my characters *are* based on real people. It's probably a dangerous thing to say, because nasty ones might not like it quite so much. But I think that any character an author writes about is probably a composite of several characters rolled into one. So that in a way they're real, but they're a mixture of several people. An awful lot of ideas that I get come from perhaps sitting on a bus or sitting in a tube train. Do you call it a tube train? Oh, a subway. Sometimes you sit there and you hear a snatch of conversation, perhaps without a beginning or an end. This sticks in your mind, and you watch people and how they behave. Yes, I think this is a kind of raw material for a writer.

Mr. Bond enjoys talking to groups of children and has often had the opportunity to meet some of his fans.

I was talking once with a group of children in a branch library in London, and a boy asked, "What did Paddington use his marmalade chunks for besides eating them?" "Oh," I said, "he used them to mark his place in books." And then I groaned to myself as I saw the librarian looking very disapproving.

One of my favorite letters is from a boy who wrote, "I like *A Bear Called Paddington* very much. I've read it 22 times. I'm thinking about buying a copy."

We had a very nice American family visit us one year. The children had been writing to me for years and years. They wrote the very first fan letter I ever had from America, and they started the Paddington Fan Club in La Jolla in California. We corresponded over the years and then their father, who is a professor in an American university, had to come to Europe for a sabbatical year. They very kindly came for half an hour and, in fact, stayed for a weekend. We had a wonderful time.

I've been writing a lot of television scripts which are seen in England, and I've been writing some books based on these characters. There's a lion called Parsley—all the characters have names of herbs. There's Parsley the lion, a dog called Dill, an owl called Sage, and they all live in an herb garden. I've written several books based on these characters, which I hope may reach America one of these days.

Had he done any writing before he began the Paddington stories?

Yes, I started writing when I was in the Army during the Second World War. I wrote short stories for adult magazines, and I wrote magazine articles, and I started writing radio plays. Then I started writing television plays. These were all for adults. *Paddington* was the first children's book I ever wrote. Since then I have been writing almost entirely for children, though I don't really think of the books as children's books. I don't really think of children's books as being any different from adult books. I think one writes as well as one can for each case.

Some Books by

MICHAEL BOND

A BEAR CALLED PADDINGTON. Illus. by Peggy Fortnum. Boston: Houghton, 1958. 128p.

At the railway station, the Browns find Paddington, a small bear who has just arrived from Darkest Peru. "Please look after this bear," pleads the sign about his neck. What else can the Browns do but invite him home with them? In a short time, Paddington has become a permanent and loved member of the family. He is a bear things happen to and the Browns soon discover that with Paddington around the house, there is never a dull moment.

HERE COMES THURSDAY. Illus. by Daphne Rowles. New York: Lothrop, 1966. 126p.

The Cupboardosities are a family of mice who live in the church organ loft and run the cheese store. When the orphan mouse Thursday balloons into their lives, he is made an hon. temp. (honorary temporary) member of the family. By the end of this first book about his adventures, Thursday has become an honorary permanent.

OLGA MEETS HER MATCH. Illus. by Hans Helweg. New York: Hastings, 1975. 128p.

Seeing that Olga is not herself, the Sawdust family decides that loneliness is the problem. As a cure, they take her to the seaside where she meets Boris Borski, another guinea pig who is as talented at storytelling as Olga is. Once at home and feeling herself again, Olga continues to enjoy her old friends and a new one, the toad Venables. Her loneliness is completely dissipated when, to her joy, she becomes a proud mother.

THE TALES OF OLGA DA POLGA. Illus. by Hans Helweg. New York: Macmillan, 1971. 144p.

When the guinea pig Olga da Polga is taken home from the pet shop to live with Karen Sawdust and her family, her exciting adventures are just beginning. Her two-room house, specially made by Mr. Sawdust, is like a palace, and in it she is visited by her new friends Noel the cat and Fangio the hedgehog. From it she is taken to a pet show where she wins a most unusual prize, and from it she ventures forth on her own to find the Elysian Fields (better known to humans as the garbage dump), so mouthwateringly described by Fangio.

Another warmly funny animal character has been created to join Paddington and Thursday.

THURSDAY AHOY! Illus. by Leslie Wood. New York: Lothrop, 1969. 130p.

Thursday and Harris have their new showboat, the S.S. *Whatsit*, loaded with passengers, food, and entertainment, and are about to sail up the river when Captain Bucket comes aboard. The debonair captain offers to sail the boat to Paradise Island where they will have a luxurious holiday. Taken in by Bucket's worldliness, they sail to Paradise, only to find themselves prisoners of SCREAM, the deadly organization whose purpose is the capture and exploitation of all mice. Thursday's ingenuity, however, saves the day, and the S.S. *Whatsit* continues its gala maiden voyage.

Other books in the Paddington series are:

MORE ABOUT PADDINGTON. Illus. by Peggy Fortnum. Boston: Houghton, 1959. 127p.

PADDINGTON ABROAD. Illus. by Peggy Fortnum. Boston: Houghton, 1972. 125p.

PADDINGTON AT LARGE. Illus by Peggy Fortnum. Boston: Houghton, 1963. 128p.

PADDINGTON AT WORK. Illus. by Peggy Fortnum. Boston: Houghton, 1967. 128p.

PADDINGTON GOES TO TOWN. Illus. by Peggy Fortnum. Boston: Houghton, 1968. 125p.

PADDINGTON HELPS OUT. Illus. by Peggy Fortnum. Boston: Houghton, 1960. 127p.

PADDINGTON MARCHES ON. Illus. by Peggy Fortnum. Boston: Houghton, 1964. 127p.

PADDINGTON TAKES THE AIR. Illus. by Peggy Fortnum. Boston: Houghton, 1970. 126p.

PADDINGTON TAKES TO TV. Illus. by Ivor Wood. Boston: Houghton, 1972. 124p.

Lucy Boston

Lucy Boston's childhood was dominated by rigidly puritanical parents. Not until she was eleven, when her family moved to the country for her mother's health, did she feel a trace of freedom from this tensely evangelical family who had stifled her sensitive spirit. There, in Westmoreland, she learned to love the outdoors and to appreciate the openness and beauty of the English countryside.

She was educated at boarding school, at a finishing school in Paris, and at Somerville, Oxford. After Oxford, she trained as a nurse in London, and then served in a French hospital during World War I. She married an English officer in the Flying Corps, and at the close of the war they returned to England. In the late 1930s she spent four years on the Continent seriously pursuing the arts. She frequented art galleries, studied painting, and visited the music centers of Europe. She wrote poetry, too, but only for herself, with no intention of having it published.

On the eve of World War II she returned to England. Her son was studying architecture at Cambridge, and she took a small apartment in the town. Then she found the place she needed. The Manor at Hemingford Grey came on the market. She had known about it in the early 1900s as a rather run-down farmhouse of ancient vintage, and when she bought it in 1939, it was still in sad condition. Not only had it been poorly cared for, but when she began to explore, she found much of its charm and ancient character hidden by added walls, false floors, and boarded up doors and fireplaces. The gardens and grounds were neglected and overgrown, almost a wilderness.

Lucy Boston's home at Hemingford Grey; the inspiration for her Green Knowe stories. Photograph by Cornelia Jones.

There are, for example, some stone walls three feet thick, Norman arched windows in those stone walls with wooden interior shutters, a small fireplace lined with ancient Roman bricks in the music room, and a huge Elizabethan fireplace in the dining room. It was there, sitting in the inglenook on winter nights, she seemed to feel the presence of those who had lived in the house long years before, and the Green Knowe stories came into being. Of her house Mrs. Boston says, "If I were a historian, a lifetime could be spent researching into it. But I just sit and talk to it. I live in it alone and find it good company."

In the thirty-odd years she has lived at Green Knowe, Mrs. Boston has fashioned beautiful gardens with annuals, perennials, and roses (some of ancient stock). She has nurtured a small apple orchard, too. But most unique are the carefully trimmed yew trees —topiaries she has designed and trimmed herself. In the dooryard are the chess set and the castle that she writes about in *The Castle of Yew*. On either side of the walk that leads to the river are large rounded yews, perfectly shaped, with the royal crown, or an animal, or a bird in flight on top of each. Her summers are devoted to her garden. Over the years she has done almost all of the work herself, aided only by a capable gardener whom she chose to employ instead of buying a car.

Her house is truly the central character of her Green Knowe books. The rooms, the furniture, the garden, the river are all just as she has so skillfully described them. Perhaps her experience as a painter has intensified her power of observation and her knowledge of colors, shapes, and textures. But her ability to describe with such striking accuracy what she sees is indicative of her talent as a writer, as is her ability to bring to life the house and all her characters, ending each story with a dramatic climax. In spite of the drama and excitement of the stories, Green Knowe retains a serenity and beauty that is also very appealing.

Mrs. Boston has often been asked if she writes for children. She replies, "My approach to children's books is to write them entirely for my own pleasure at my own age. Perhaps I got stuck at age eleven."

In 1961 Mrs. Boston was awarded the Carnegie Medal for *A Stranger at Green Knowe*, and in 1969 she received the Lewis Carroll Shelf Award for *The Children at Green Knowe*.

She has written a fascinating and sometimes humorous account of her life at Green Knowe in *Memory in a House* (Macmillan, 1973). For a longer critical account of Mrs. Boston's life and writing see, also, *Lucy Boston, a Walck Monograph*, by Jasper Rose (Walck, 1966).

Interview

Many have asked me whether the children of Green Knowe who came from the past were real. That is the leading question. How do we know whether they were or not? We don't really know who lived in the house. Anybody might have. I always have the very strong feeling of children about the house, particularly sitting in the inglenook 'round the fire when I am alone there in the evening. They just come into my head. They may have been there or they may not have been there. I've also been asked whether any of the incidents in any of the stories really happened. I don't know whether they did or they didn't. They could have. Tolly is a portrait of my son as a little boy, as near as I could make it. A good many people think that I am Mrs. Oldknow, but I'm not nearly so nice.

Mrs. Boston answered some questions our children asked about a few of her books.

The little flowers that I describe in *The Children of Green Knowe* are all flowers that I grow in my garden. When they come in winter, they are mostly sticks with little buds on them which suddenly open and do look rather magical. The tiny roses which Tolly bought for a Christmas present for his grandmother are roses you can buy anywhere. They do smell as much as big roses, and are about three inches high when you buy them. Unfortunately, they soon grow into large rose trees with tiny flowers on them. Then they don't look so interesting. They are not dollhouse roses anymore.

I chose a gorilla in *A Stranger at Green Knowe* because I saw a photo of him which was so like a man that I thought I must go and see what kind of animal this was. It was because he was so like a man that he was so interesting. I thought it was so wicked that he should be in such a tiny cage—too small to move in, and shut up absolutely alone for the whole of his life as he is, with no mate and no company. I thought it would make a very moving story.

In An Enemy at Green Knowe *there is a great deal about witches and witchcraft. Did you already know a lot or was it necessary for you to learn about it?*

I had to learn about it. I got all the books I could from the university library and read them. If there was not enough witchcraft to suit my purposes, I invented it. I do not know about any spell where you have to nail the skin of a child's hand to the front door with curses. I made that up.

Did the story of THE CASTLE OF YEW *take place at Green Knowe?*

The castles are there and the whole chess set. A great many children come and try to get small enough to go into the castle. I haven't seen anybody succeed yet. The nests are inside.

Why did you stop writing the Green Knowe books and write THE SEA EGG?

Somebody sent me a sea egg as a present, just with a little letter saying "We thought you'd like this." At once, at the sight of it, the story came into my head, and I couldn't resist writing it. I enjoyed writing it more than anything I have ever written. It takes place in Kynance Cove in Cornwall, which has a tunnel and an island and all the necessary things. It's where I have stayed often and I love it particularly.

The illustrator of the Green Knowe books is my son. Since he was Tolly, he is better qualified than anybody else to draw all the toys which were his own, and the things in the house which he's known all his life. The toy box was his, for instance. Of course, he knows this house well, even though he wasn't brought up in it, and he can draw. He's an architect.

When I am writing, the important part of each story pours out. Tiny details take a lot of thought, hold me up sometimes for weeks because it's very difficult to get all the things you want to happen happening in the number of days necessary for the story. There is always some reason why the story has to take place in a certain number of days. It's very hard to arrange that. But apart from that, the story and the characters and the things that happen come fully fledged into my mind, and I've only got to sit down and write them. It's as easy as that. It's the details that are difficult. I do a great deal of revising to get the English how I want it. The first time you write it down very often you say too much, or sometimes you say too little. It has to be improved. It has to be enlarged. I'm very fussy about the English. The book I enjoyed writing most was *The Sea Egg*, as I have said. It took only about three weeks. It just wrote itself. I was very, very happy about it, but I think actually my best book is *A Stranger at Green Knowe*.

Some Books by
LUCY BOSTON

THE CASTLE OF YEW. Illus. by Margery Gill. New York: Harcourt, 1965. 58p.

Joseph has seen the garden at Green Knowe through the fence and the honeysuckle, but often thought he would like to go in. When the mailman asks him to deliver the mail to Mrs. Oldknow's door, he knows he can ask permission to look around. "You can go anywhere you want, if you really want to," she tells him. After he walks around the garden, he examines the yew tree that is clipped in the shape of a castle, and sees that it has windows and a door, rooms and a stairway inside. He walks his fingers through the door and suddenly, there he is, the size of a finger, standing in the cobbled hall. He is not alone. Robin, a boy from the village, is there, too.

Together their life in the castle seems so real that children who read the book will hope that someday it will happen to them.

THE CHILDREN OF GREEN KNOWE. Illus. by Peter Boston. New York: Harcourt, 1955. 157p.

Young Tolly is excited about going to live with his great-grandmother. He's never seen her before, but he imagines she is very old. When he meets her, he barely notices that she is very small and bent, has white hair and heavy wrinkles in her face. She seems to know what small boys like, and Tolly knows on his first night there that he will be happy at Green Knowe. Granny often tells Tolly stories about the three children in the picture that hangs over the large fireplace: Alexander and Toby and Linnet, their six-year-old sister. They lived in this house long years ago, but some of their playthings are still there. As the days pass, it seems to Tolly that the children are there with him in the house, that he hears their voices and sees them playing in the garden.

Reality and fantasy are skillfully blended to create this enchanting story. It is the first of five Green Knowe books.

AN ENEMY AT GREEN KNOWE. Illus. by Peter Boston. New York: Harcourt, 1964. 156p.

The summer that Ping and Tolly spend together at Green Knowe, Granny holds them spellbound with her stories of Dr. Vogel, the mad scientist who came to the Manor House in 1630 as a tutor for Roger Oldknow, but practiced alchemy and black magic in secret. Later that summer, an odd, unpleasant stranger, Miss Melanie Powers, comes to live in the neighborhood. She is in search of certain old manuscripts written by Dr. Vogel, and she believes the papers are still at Green Knowe. By weird and devious methods, including witchcraft and black magic, she attempts to gain possession, not only of Dr. Vogel's papers, but of Green Knowe itself. The boys work desperately to protect their beloved Granny and Green Knowe from the several plagues that descend upon them.

This is a highly imaginative story in which the suspense is skillfully sustained from beginning to end.

NOTHING SAID. Illus. by Peter Boston. New York: Harcourt, 1971. 64p.

When Libby goes to spend a week in the home of her mother's friend, Julia, she has no idea what an enchanting place Julia's home will be. The house is old and rambling. The garden borders on a river with a footpath running along its banks. There are great trees hanging over the water, and little pools hollowed out by the current. A large elm spreads its branches over the largest and deepest pool. Julia's dog, Cobweb, barks furiously at a picture of nymphs bathing in that pool. Has he seen them in the river? Does he know them? Libby's week is filled with wonder and adventure, particularly her encounter in the moonlight the last night of her visit—is it a dream or a reality? Libby can never be sure.

THE RIVER AT GREEN KNOWE. Illus. by Peter Boston. New York: Harcourt, 1959. 153p.

Ida, Oscar, and Ping can't imagine a more perfect place to be for a summer vacation than Green Knowe. They don't know each other until they arrive as guests of Dr. Maud Biggin, who had rented the house from Mrs. Oldknow for the summer. In a canoe which they find in the boathouse, the three children explore the river and its islands by day and night. Each day brings them adventures more exciting than anything they could ever imagine, and their nightly exploits are strange and magical. On some of their adventures they meet a gentle giant and his mother from a past age, see flying horses, and explore an ancient deserted mansion.

THE SEA EGG. Illus. by Peter Boston. New York: Harcourt, 1967. 94p.
Toby and Joe want the beautiful egg-shaped stone that Sam, the lobster man, has shown them. They call it a sea egg, and when it is theirs, they place it in a secluded tidal pool at the end of a rock tunnel, where the sea cannot wash it away and it won't be disturbed by people. Later, when they discover a baby triton in their pool, their joy is unbounded. The three play together constantly, unconscious of time. Always learning from the triton, the boys lose all fear of the sea, ride the waves, swim underwater, explore the tunnels and rock caves along the shore. The last night of their holiday, the little triton takes Joe and Toby on a most amazing adventure—one that dreams are made of, but one so real that forever they will believe in their little companion of the sea.

A STRANGER AT GREEN KNOWE. Illus. by Peter Boston. New York: Harcourt, 1961. 158p.
Shortly after the Chinese boy, Ping, comes to spend the summer at Green Knowe with Mrs. Oldknow, the newspapers and radio announce the escape of Hanno, a giant gorilla, from the London Zoo. Ping is deeply disturbed for he has seen Hanno in the zoo and has a great sympathy for this magnificent animal confined in such a small cage and stared at by thousands of people. Ping longs to find Hanno, bring him to the wood at Green Knowe, and secretly protect him from his pursuers. Carefully Ping makes his plans, and for a few short days his hopes are realized.
      This is a moving story which presents a powerful case for the wild caged animals. Awarded Carnegie Medal in 1961.

THE TREASURE OF GREEN KNOWE. Illus. by Peter Boston. New York: Harcourt, 1958. 185p.
Tolly returns to Green Knowe for his spring holiday wondering what he will find. Will it be different from the Green Knowe he remembers from his last holiday there? When he arrives, the picture of Toby, Alexander, and Linnet is gone. Mrs. Oldknow has loaned it for an exhibit. Tolly is beside himself. He can't imagine what Green Knowe will be like without them. Their picture has been

replaced by one of Maria Oldknow, wife of Captain Oldknow and mistress of this house in the late eighteenth century. Each evening by the fireside as Granny mends a quilt made of clothes of Maria's family, she tells Tolly stories of blind Susan and her devoted friend Jacob, of the great fire at Green Knowe, and of the strange disappearance of Maria's jewels. As Tolly listens to the stories, he learns to know this family as he had known Toby and Alexander and Linnet. They move in and out of Tolly's days at Green Knowe like shadow people, seeming very real and close to him at times. The story builds to an unusual climax at the end of Tolly's holiday, and during his last day at Green Knowe he has the most exciting adventure of all.

This sequel to *The Children of Green Knowe* continues to build interest in the house and in those who might have lived there.

Pauline Clarke. Photo courtesy of Ms. Clarke.

Pauline Clarke

Pauline Clarke has written poetry, fantasy, and historical fiction for children. Her range reflects the variety of her interests. She is best known in the United States for *The Return of the Twelves*, for which she received the Carnegie Medal, and *The Five Dolls* books (now out of print), written under the pseudonym of Helen Clare.

Miss Clarke was born in Nottinghamshire and went to school in London and Essex. She studied English literature at Somerville College, Oxford. Later she became a journalist and worked on a children's magazine. Since 1949 she has done free-lance writing for both adults and children. After she went to live with an artist friend, Cecil Leslie, whose household included several Pekingese dogs, she wrote a book about the dogs for Miss Leslie to illustrate. Many of Miss Clarke's other books are also illustrated by Miss Leslie, including the English edition of *The Return of the Twelves*. Miss Clarke has adapted her own stories and has authored educational materials for the BBC in England. She often lectures on children's books and the writing of children's materials.

In 1963 she directed a seminar for the British Council in Accra. The purpose of the conference was to instruct native teachers to write children's stories in English with African settings.

It was while Miss Clarke was doing research for her book *Torolv, the Fatherless* that she met her husband, an authority on Anglo-Saxon history. They now live in Cambridge, where he is a fellow of Emmanuel College.

Interview

> *Miss Clarke discusses the Brontë children and the stories they wrote called* THE HISTORY OF THE YOUNG MEN, *on which she based her book* THE RETURN OF THE TWELVES.

You have to remember that the games the Brontë children played with their soldiers came before the stories. You must imagine the four of them in the family in Yorkshire: Branwell, the oldest and a boy, Charlotte, Emily, and Ann, getting together in a tiny little room which you can still see if you go to Haworth—a little room above the porch—playing these wonderful games with this set of soldiers. Branwell had had various sets of soldiers before, but these seem to be very special, these Twelves. He had them in 1826 when he was eight years old. He describes how his father bought them for him and how each of the girls chose one for her own. They worked a very special game with these Twelves. They worked out this idea of being their genii, or guardian angels. Each child had a particular soldier that was hers or his. You can imagine them in this little room having very rowdy games, I think. Branwell was the ringleader, with battles and adventures and sea voyages and journeys. They had, in fact, a set of ninepins which they pretended were cannibals, and they would launch these, we can imagine, against the soldiers and have fights between the two. The genii would then swoop down and rescue their own soldiers and look after them. Branwell himself had red hair, and when he came to write the story, he made one of these strange creatures, these genii, have a red halo, and we know that this is what he is referring to—his red hair.

Well, above all you can imagine them making a terrific noise. I'm sure they did. I'm sure they were very much more natural children, as little children, than we sometimes think—this Brontë family. The noise was sometimes terrific. One time Tabby, the cook, who looked after them, called in her nephew from the street because she thought they'd all gone mad.

Branwell made up a special language for his soldiers, and he's said to have done it (I can't remember where I read this, but it is, in fact, stated somewhere) by speaking in bold Yorkshire and holding his nose at the same time. He wrote a rather strange little language for them, too. It was a mixture of English and French with bits of Greek letters in it as well. The children invented this idea of wooden soldiers coming alive again when they got killed because, of course, the soldiers can't be killed off permanently. Well, if you can imagine, all that was going on as they grew from their early years when they were six and seven and eight, until about 1830 when Branwell was twelve, and then I suppose the soldiers were perhaps lost.

The Brontës were getting older, and they had an absorbing interest in writing and began to write down the stories of the soldiers. They brought in all the games they had played and expanded them, made them bigger and more detailed. They wrote them in tiny little books with tiny pens and wee writing (they made it look like printing), I think partly because they had the idea that this was the proper scale for the soldiers and partly, no doubt, to save paper.

Branwell put all the games into the writing. He had imagined that these twelve soldiers had set off to Africa in a ship called *The Invincible*, and they were going to carve themselves out a kingdom amongst the Ashantis in Africa. He tells all this in *The History of the Young Men*. They built towns, twelve towns. They had parliaments. They had constant battles and excitements, visits of the genii in the desert. And when the Twelves, or Young Men, as they called them, got settled, the Brontës even started to write a series of magazines for them. They called them the *Young Men's Magazines*, with poems and stories and articles all about their life in Africa. You can see these whenever you go to the museum in their home in Haworth. These tiny little books are only twice the size of an English penny (3½ inches tall). There are lots more stories other than *The History of the Young Men*, and quite a few are written by Charlotte as well as Branwell. The whole series are called the Angria stories because they called this country Angria instead of Africa. Branwell's are the liveliest stories, and Charlotte's are more romantic. I use Branwell's mostly as background, especially for the characters of the twelve soldiers.

Miss Clarke discusses the techniques of writing fantasy. In THE RETURN OF THE TWELVES *each soldier has a unique personality. Miss Clarke explains how she developed their personalities.*

Their characters and their looks are very clearly described by Branwell in all his stories, and I simply tried to develop the outlines and the ideas that he gave. I'd like to read his list of their names and their ages from *The History of the Young Men*. Here it is: "Butter Crashey, captain, age 140 years; Alexander Cheeky, surgeon, age 20 years; Arthur Wellesley, trumpeter, 12; William Edward Parry, trumpeter, 15; Alexander Sneaky, sailor, 17; John Rose, lieutenant, 16; William Bravey, sailor, 27; Edward Gravey, sailor, 17; Stumps, 12, middy (that means midshipman); Monkey, 11, middy; Tracky, 10, middy; Crackey, 5, middy." Charlotte has rather different sailors, but I stuck to Branwell's mainly because he is very good at developing their characters and telling you about them. For instance, he goes on to say, "Crashey, the captain, was a patriarch, full of years and full of wisdom. Cheeky was the most stouthearted man in the ship. A. Sneaky was ingenious, artful, deceitful, but courageous; J. Ross, frank, open, honest, and of a bravery, when in battle, sometimes approaching to madness. W. Bravey was of a character similar to Ross, but his countenance and habits seemed to like to say 'Give us good cheer. Eat, drink, dance, and be merry.' Different from these was the character of Edward Gravey. He was naturally grave and melancholy, and his temper was still further soured by the sneers and laughter which the rest raised against him, but like the rest he was daring and brave. Of the other four midshipmen I need not speak particularly. Suffice it to say that like other middies they were merry, thoughtless, liked sport, and cared not for the future." Well, that's what Branwell says about his soldiers, and he adds a great deal to that throughout the stories.

What I tried to do was simply to develop this and use his ideas. I can give you some examples of this. It was quite easy to make Butter Crashey wise and alert and dignified with this wonderfully dignified, rather Biblical language, and cool and benign because he's very clearly drawn, not at all difficult to follow. Now Gravey is a good character. Branwell makes comic and yet disastrous things happen to Gravey. He always seems to have disasters that are rather funny happening to him. For instance, he's swept overboard with the mast in a sea battle. So, I followed this idea and made rather disastrous comic things always happen to Gravey. I also developed the notion of his being rather melancholy, which is why he is called Gravey, of course. Now, Sneaky was Branwell's own soldier, and he's like his name. He's artful and rather jealous, and he counsels treachery when they are discussing their advances on the Ashantis. He's very cocksure. He actually, in the Parliament, proposes himself as the king. This was easy to follow, too. I made him into a kind of ringleader, a rather envious person and full of himself. Stumps is another rather important character in my book because Max is so fond of him. Stumps in Branwell's stories is constantly dying and being made alive and coming back and disappearing. You never can quite keep track of Stumps, so this is why I let him get lost in the kitchen and also be swept off the raft and drowned, or not quite drowned, in the river. Stumps is a very lovable and solid character in Branwell's stories, and I tried to develop this. These are just some examples of how I've tried to do it with all of them, really.

> *The soldiers had a very exciting march to Haworth. Miss Clarke and her illustrator together worked out the route of the march.*

I did the march back to Haworth from maps and photos and imagination and from memory. I had been there in 1953 and I wrote the book, I suppose, in 1961-62, but I must tell you that the artist had a part here, too. She wanted very much to go to Haworth to get the feeling of the countryside before she began all the pictures, even though in the English edition she wasn't going to have very much space to draw a countryside. She also wanted to (and felt she must) see Branwell's own paintings and drawings of his soldiers which are in the museum at Haworth. So, while she was at Haworth, she actually walked out that march for me and in one particular she corrected it. When she saw Branwell's drawings, very faded watercolors of the soldiers, she noticed that some of the soldiers were wearing feathers in their caps in his drawings, and they were carrying a flag in a battle. This is why I let them pick out the feathers they found in the straw stack and wear those feathers, and why I gave them a flag.

Max's life with his family and his life with the soldiers are so skillfully juxtaposed that at no time does the reader question the reality of either. Miss Clarke discusses how she accomplished this.

This was not difficult exactly, but I had to feel my way. As each new child and finally the one adult, Mr. Howson, was let into the secret, I was conscious of it becoming more and more delicate to keep up the belief in the magic. You have to build up a totally convincing real setting, and then your reader will believe anything. If my characters, Max and the others, are real enough to you when you read the book, then whatever fantastic happenings come to Max will be believed. This sounds a contradiction, but I think it's at the bottom of good fantasy—to make your real setting so real that it grips the reader, and then he will believe what you tell him.

Although I tried to make the whole family real, I never let the parents openly into the secret, you notice, though Mrs. Morley is sympathetic to some strangeness that she feels is going on, and is very sympathetic to Max's feeling for his soldiers. Now, the adult who is let in, Mr. Howson, knows all about the Brontës and is very sympathetic to the whole idea. I don't think I could have kept up the reality if I'd let everyone into full enjoyment of the secret. I let the whole neighborhood get excited when the two little girls said they had seen the soldiers in the corn, but I only told this. I didn't show the grown-ups actually searching at firsthand or discussing it much. You can tell more than you can show in this kind of situation. I think to show the soldiers alive in the museum in public would have been a mistake, perhaps not believable. They had this useful freezing habit to outsiders. They went dead, they froze when they needed to. That is to say that some will see them alive and some won't. Imagination is just this—it's seeing more than your neighbor sees—sometimes. Children have it particularly.

Now the Twelves themselves know that they must freeze at times and they keep to this rule. There's an occasion when Butter is on the mantle shelf, having been brought back and found by the farmer, and the children stand around wondering what will happen. "He and Jane and Philip all stood silently gazing at the patriarch, each thinking the same thing—'What would happen if Crashey, recognizing the genii's voices, should hold up his tiny arms and then bow and smile and speak to them?' " Well, of course, Crashey knows perfectly well that there are outsiders in the room and he does no such thing. It doesn't happen; it doesn't arise. He stays frozen, and this is an important and useful part of keeping the fantasy going.

Then there was the very important question of scale. I never forgot scale. It was never out of my mind. The soldier's-eye view had to be given in detail. It had to be made as real as the human's. You alter the focus, but you alter it accurately all the time from one setting to the other. There is an occasion again when Butter is in the farmer's pocket and he describes how he finds himself in this dark, smelly hammock with what looks like a piece of old sheet which is, of course, a handkerchief, and what looks like a stake as long as himself, which is a nail, and a long coil of rope, which is a piece of string. That is a little example of doing it from a soldier's-eye view, and this has to be done constantly and never to be forgotten.

I built up the liveliness of the toys themselves in various ways. I did it partly by this wonderful difference, this individuality, which Branwell had already given them in looks and characters. Partly, I think, they have life because of their very antiqueness and their old-fashioned talk (both the very dignified Biblical talk of the patriarch, and the rather rowdy, swashbuckling talk of the people like Bravey). It's all old-fashioned. It's something rather individual. Then very importantly, very much a part of their life and their character—which Max himself realizes—is that they had to do things for themselves. When Philip has made a plan to get them back into the museum, he says it's a good plan because they can do it with dignity and they can also do it under their own steam. This is very important to Max, for he'd realized quite early that part of their life depended on their being left to do things by themselves and not being interfered with. He could oversee and suggest but not dictate. The soldiers had undertaken the whole march without consulting him. I think that this is a point which adds to their reality.

I think that you get this sixth sense as to what you can get away with, what the rules are for any particular story, as you write. You get it by being completely absorbed in the story and sure of it yourself. You're there. You're in the pocket with Crashey, and you're in the moonlit yard with Max and Stumps, you're in the museum waiting with Philip. And this is how you alter the focus. There's no other way to do it. You feel your way, like Max imagining what his soldiers are doing as he lies in bed. That chapter is meant to be a parallel about his imagining what goes on. So, it is a very delicate operation with its own rules which you have to feel for.

The *Five Dolls* books, which I wrote under the name of Helen Clare, have their own rules, too. There are no grown-ups in person in those books at all. They are only referred to. They're only talked about, as is Elizabeth's brother Edward. Elizabeth is the little girl who can get small enough to go into her doll's house. All the action takes place amongst toys—toy trains, toy castles, a toy zoo. It's a toy world. The doll's house exists in its own small world and the great real world is always there for Elizabeth to come from and go back to. The real world is talked about, but it doesn't really come into the stories; although, all the things the dolls do are simply what children do in real life. From this point of view the doll books are sheer realism. The dolls go to weddings, they go to fetes, and they have picnics. They help in the house or the garden, they do the washing, they do the spring cleaning. It is just life from a doll's-eye view.

Miss Clarke finds writing realistic stories just as interesting and satisfying as writing imaginative stories.

I think each kind of story has its own kind of satisfaction. Also, they're not so very different. You've got to make a real setting and real characters, whether you're writing fantasy or a real life story. Otherwise, the setting and characters won't stand out, they won't be real at all, or convincing. Imaginative stories are very freeing; they're very releasing to the writer because, in effect, you have this feeling of having a godlike power to make anything happen that you fancy.

I remember once writing a short story, and greatly enjoying it, about an Oriental prince, a schoolboy prince, who went to spend

Christmas with one of his school friends in London. The family took him shopping for presents at various big London stores. He arranged a snowstorm in one of the stores, and made the taxi that they were in take off from a traffic jam like a helicopter. In the end, he flew away on the hall carpet, accompanied by the chancellor from his country who had come to fetch him.

Making anything like this happen is tremendous fun. But in practice you find that every situation in a fantasy has its own rules and its own logic, and if the author doesn't keep to them, the story will break down. The story needs to be anchored in good reality to convince any but the very youngest child. I suppose that the very young child's notion of reality is nothing like as rigid as ours. Anyway, the line between fantasy and reality is so cloudy. We all have fantasies—young and old. But realistic stories have another kind of satisfaction. They have the satisfaction of describing the everyday truthfully, yet making it just that much larger than life, to be exciting, inspiring, or harrowing. That is, to make the everyday shine, as it does sometimes in reality, with promise or with warmth or with comedy, or sometimes even with a visionary quality.

In historical stories I get great pleasure and satisfaction from building up a picture of a past time with countless tiny details— social details about clothes and kitchens, and cooking and daily life, and ships and armies and buildings. Of course, you never really know how close your picture is to the real one. You never can know this about earlier times. You can only aim at making it a total and convincing picture, after doing your research as widely as you can. I have written two historical stories. One is called *Torolv the Fatherless*, which is a story about Anglo-Saxons and Vikings, and its climax is the Battle of Maldon on the Essex coast in 991. Its theme is the conflict of loyalties between the boy, Torolv, who comes to England with the Vikings, gets left behind accidently, and is looked after by the Saxons. Then he finds his former lord fighting with his present lord, and he's in a great conflict.

Then I've written another story about the Henry V period called *The Boy with the Erpingham Hood*, which has the Battle of Agincourt in it and various other stirring deeds.

In really fast-moving, realistic stories—such as thrillers, for instance—there is a great satisfaction (though a dreadful head-ache) in working out a tightly connected plot with all the strands really dovetailing and working together. Really, plot is always the most taxing part of making a story, but in a thriller it's perhaps more difficult than in other kinds of stories that move more slowly. Family stories, for instance, may go from incident to incident rather gently.

Of all my books, I think *Torolov, the Fatherless* is really my fa-vorite.[1] I don't quite know why except that I've always been very devoted to that period of history, and it seems to me to be the most shapely book I've written. I think I almost enjoyed it more than any. But it is difficult to say that because one really enjoys each book as one is doing it, and each book is a different experi-ence, of course.

Some Books by
PAULINE CLARKE

THE RETURN OF THE TWELVES. Illus. by Bernarda Bryson. New York: Coward, 1963. 252p.

> In his *History of the Young Men*, Branwell Brontë recorded stories which the Brontë children made up as they played with a set of twelve wooden soldiers. Imagining what might have happened had these soldiers been found years later, Pauline Clarke brings them to life again in this fantasy.
>
> Awarded the Carnegie Medal, 1963.

THE TWO FACES OF SILENUS. New York: Coward, 1972. 160p.

> While staying in a small Italian hill town, Rufus and Drusilla Green-wood meet magic and adventure when they throw coins into an ancient fountain and make a wish. The statue of Silenus, son of Pan, comes to life, and strange and magical events take place. The giant, shaggy-haired creature brings garlands of flowers to Dru, and the

---

1. *Torolov, the Fatherless* was never published in the United States.

flowers never wither. At his command, two stone lions come to life. Medusa, the personification of evil, comes disguised and turns the children into stone, and later, they are transformed into animals. The dramatic events pile one upon another and lead to a tremendous climax, before Silenus is once again returned to stone.

The Five Dolls books mentioned by Miss Clarke are no longer in print:

FIVE DOLLS AND THE DUKE. Prentice-Hall, 1968. unp. o.p.

FIVE DOLLS AND THE MONKEY. Prentice-Hall, 1967. unp. o.p.

FIVE DOLLS AND THEIR FRIENDS. Prentice-Hall, 1966. unp. o.p.

FIVE DOLLS IN A HOUSE. Prentice-Hall, 1965. unp. o.p.

FIVE DOLLS IN THE SNOW. Prentice-Hall, 1967. unp. o.p.

Penelope Farmer. Photo courtesy of Atheneum Publishers.

Penelope Farmer

Penelope Farmer was born in Kent just before World War II. Because of the flying bombs that plagued the area, her earliest memories are of waking in the night to the sound of bombs overhead. It was, she says, "a rather muddled early childhood."

With the end of the war, her childhood became more normal. Her family, which included her parents, a twin sister, an older brother, and a younger sister, lived in the country and always had animals about. She tried writing animal stories "in the manner of Beatrix Potter," and she and her twin sister wrote and put on puppet plays. Her full-time hobby, however, was reading.

Miss Farmer studied history at Oxford University and did graduate work in social studies at London University. She has done all kinds of work, including teaching for a year in the East End of London. She had a book of adult stories published and a television play produced before she began to write for children.

Miss Farmer and her husband have remodeled an old house in London, where they live now with their two young children.

Interview

> *Penelope Farmer has written several fantasies whose themes vary, but whose two main characters, Charlotte and Emma, remain constant. The first book,* THE SUMMER BIRDS, *tells of the wonder-struck summer when a sometimes invisible boy teaches the girls to fly.*

I don't really find the idea of children learning to fly so unusual. There's *Peter Pan*, which is one of the first stories any child in this country gets to know about. It seems to me it's one of the most obvious things—that children want to be able to fly, and they think about it and occasionally dream about it. I wrote *The Summer Birds* first as a very short story when I was about seventeen or eighteen. I think it was very much a part of the way I was thinking and dreaming.

Why did I give the boy the ability to make himself invisible? I don't know. I think it's just that I didn't want people to notice him. It was not so much invisibility. It was just that somehow he had the ability to make himself not noticed by people.

Up to a point, yes, I do plan a book in detail. I think you have to. I have to make up an outline from the point of view of publishing it, for the mechanics and that sort of thing. I have to make up a synopsis to send to the publisher, anyway. This, I find, is a very useful discipline, but I don't necessarily stick to the synopsis. It's there, giving me a kind of kicking-off point. Very often you find the whole plot changes. Things happen in the plot which could never have happened before you've actually written a part of it. In some instances the plot naturally springs from what you've written, where it probably wouldn't have occurred to you before. It comes spontaneously, all at once. You get an idea, and it is just a little silly thing, and it might sound very insignificant and unimportant. It grows gradually bit by bit. You walk down the street and you see something that gives you another idea. You add it in, or you may not. You may find you want to add it in but it doesn't quite fit, and you fiddle around with it and you fiddle around with it. Finally, somehow, it slides into place in the plot, or it doesn't and you chuck it out. You must always allow for this; you must allow for things developing. Sometimes the things that develop are

much better than the original, sort of mechanical, setting-out of
the plot.

I don't know how I create my characters. You have sometimes
preconceptions about a character as somebody you know whom
you want to use, or anyway start off with. But very often the
character just grows in the course of writing a book. You bring a
character in. Sometimes you're consciously developing a character. Sometimes they sort of develop themselves, and sometimes the
development is part of the structure of the book. The book may
need a certain kind of character to balance the others. This is self-
conscious, even though to a large extent the character is developing
unconsciously, subconsciously. This is something you feel. It is
sort of a feeling of balance and contrast.

Practically any character is difficult to write about. Probably
you only understand them inasmuch as they have certain elements
of you in them. So you're starting with different facets of your own
character and using them to build up someone separate, distinct. I
think the most difficult characters are always the ones you're looking at from the outside all the time. Sometimes it's much easier; you
can set a character with a couple of sentences, and it works very
well. But I think one of my most difficult characters was Bobby
Fumpkins, the fat boy in *Emma in Winter*. This had to be a creation
in a sense. The other characters I was thinking through all the time,
but he had to build up. He started off as a subsidiary character,
and I sort of built him up to round him out. I had difficulties. To
what extent I succeeded I still don't know. I didn't always feel that
I'd perhaps rounded him out well enough, because he was more
deliberately created, in a way, than the other characters.

Charlotte and Emma are very much based on my mother and
her sister as little girls. They were rather in the same situation,
with no parents and having to be everything to each other. One of
them was very much the responsible one and protected her sister,
who was rather difficult. Emma and Charlotte have grown in their
own ways and aren't exactly based on my mother and her sister
now, but this is where it started.

I have another book about Charlotte, the older of the two sisters
in *The Summer Birds*. It's called *Charlotte Sometimes*. It's a completely different setting. It's in a boarding school which is set very
near where I live in London. It's a very complicated plot, and it's

rather difficult to explain it in the abstract. She lands back in time, in the same school, but in 1918 during the First World War. It goes backwards and forwards between the two periods. Anyway, that's the beginning of the germ of the plot.

I find it very difficult to talk about any book which I am currently involved with. I can look at *The Summer Birds* and say it was about so and so, and this happened and that happened, because that was a long time ago. But with a book that I've only just finished, I find that a synopsis sounds very bare and bald and stupid. If you've been living with it for a long time, it's so familiar to you and you know it so well that it sounds completely unoriginal and completely boring, and you have no confidence in it. But once a book's been out and everyone's seen it and knows the main idea as well as you do, you're not so embarrassed about talking about it.

I live in London now, but I grew up in the country in Kent on the North Downs, and we often went to the South Downs. I've a great feel for this country. It's very bare and bony and old, and I love it. The settings of *The Summer Birds* and *Emma in Winter* are in this area. The settings were built up from elements in different places but aren't one specific place. *Sea Gull* is set in Wiltshire, another part of the south of England which is a lot different. They're inland downs as opposed to downs by the sea. That is the one book which is based in a very, very specific area—you know, the topography and all that. It's one place that I love very much. We used to go and stay with friends who had a house there. I liked this and I wanted to use it for a setting, and I did. The house is still there. It's been taken over by someone who doesn't really have any feeling for the character of the house at all but fills the garden with very fat plastic gnomes. We still go and look at it, and the countryside is lovely just the same. I'd like perhaps someday to set another book there, but this hasn't so far happened.

I started writing for children because I was asked to. I wrote a book of short stories when I was very young and still at school. They were published in England, and they were neither for adults nor for children. They were a collection of sort of fairy stories. Margaret McElderry of Harcourt, Brace read them. She didn't think she could find a market for it in the States but said they would like to commission me to do a children's book. I started from there really.

I always wrote, but I didn't usually finish things. The short stories were sort of a confidence booster. They've just been re-issued in this country, so I've been looking at them again and I shudder all the time. I'm looking at them now through an extremely critical eye. They seem to me incredibly naively written, but I think from an outsider's point of view they probably work. I couldn't write in that way now. I got away with it because that was the way I was thinking at the time I wrote them. If I tried to write like that now, it would be horrible. I do probably sometimes let that kind of phrasing escape now, but I go through the story pruning it very radically. You do change as a writer, I think, inevitably. You become much more self-conscious. And much more self-critical. This can be weakening and very inhibiting. But you must achieve a balance between being inhibited by it and helped by it.

I don't write for any particular age group. I have to occasionally because there is a series of books in this country which I have written for, and occasionally I write for radio for a specific age range. But when I sit down and write a long novel, one of the things I really start entirely because I want to do it, not because anyone asks me to do it, then I just write it as it comes and let the publishers decide. I don't write a book for children, I write a book; and this is a big distinction, I think. If you start off saying, "Well, an eight-year-old might take that, but I don't think he'd take that," then you'd just write a bad book in any terms. I do think you've got to set up a sort of scale of age in your mind. You do a little thing in the back of your brain, saying, "No, leave it out. That's too much. That's too sophisticated." But it's not a very conscious thing. It's there in the background, but you forget about it totally. Once you start writing, you find that once you've created a style of writing, the thing goes on from there. You know, the thing has its own coherence, its own form. You somehow don't exceed the limits that you've set yourself.

I've started to write with an artist and we find we work very well together. We are doing a joint project making picture books from Greek myths. We are starting off with the story of Daedalus and Icarus and the story of Cadmus and the dragon's teeth. He's illustrating them and I'm writing them. All the time we're working very closely together. He's looking at the stories and saying, "I can't illustrate that. Cut that thing. It doesn't work." I look at the illustrations and say, "No, I don't think that can work." It's most exciting because he'll say something, and I can take it a little bit further, and he can take it a little bit further still. Or I've got something half formulated in my mind, and he will pick it up and sort of develop it for me so that I can then take it on from there. What makes this still more exciting is that we're simultaneously working on some film versions of these stories, using the drawings and the scripts.

When you are a writer, you work very much by yourself, shut up in a little room. You get very inward-looking and depressed by what you're doing, and it's all totally related to yourself. Being a writer can be incredibly lonely sometimes. But I balance it by this kind of project, which is very good. It's quite a different process from writing by yourself. It's very exciting, although as a writer, one is still bound to write a great deal on one's own and do things in which only you are involved.

Some Books by
PENELOPE FARMER

A CASTLE OF BONE. New York: Atheneum, 1972. 151p.
Hugh's friend Anna had just closed Hugh's leather wallet into the cupboard when a squealing pig burst through the cupboard door and careened down the stairs and out into the park. Hugh and his father had bought the cupboard in an old junk shop, and the wallet was the first thing that had gone into it. A few experiments showed that anything placed there went back to its beginnings: a box of matches became a small tree, a brass button came out as two pieces of rock. It was all fun and mysterious and only slightly frightening until Penn, Hugh's friend, was accidentally pushed into the cupboard and emerged as a baby. It might have been funny but it wasn't; it was horrible. The final effort to return Penn to himself is fraught with danger and terror.

CHARLOTTE SOMETIMES. Illus. by Chris Connor. New York: Harcourt, 1969. 192p.

Charlotte is in her first term at boarding school when she finds herself transposed in time and person. It is 1918, her name is Clare, and the girl Emily in the next bed seems to be her sister. The days that follow are exhausting and incomprehensible, as she alternates between the past and the present, between being Clare and being Charlotte. She is frightened and anxious when the interchanges suddenly stop and she is caught in the past. As the weeks pass by, she despairs of finding her way back to the present and is dismayed to realize that she can hardly remember what it was like to be Charlotte. When the opportunity to return finally occurs, she seizes it and is then able to unravel the mystery of Clare.

EMMA IN WINTER. Illus. by James J. Spanfeller. New York: Harcourt, 1966. 160p.

With her sister Charlotte away at boarding school, Emma finds herself lonely and miserable and with no real friends at all. Only Bobby Fumpkins seems anxious to be friendly, and who wants to be friends with stupid Baby Fumpkins? When her nightmarish dreams begin, Emma is at first alone in them, flying with great difficulty over the snow-covered downs in the cold darkness of night. It is not until the third dream that she senses that something else is there, a frightening presence with huge glittering eyes. Then she becomes aware of someone else in her dream, someone whose round face and awkward flight soon identify him as the despised Bobby Fumpkins. In every dream, he clumsily struggles to reach her as she mocks him and laughs at him. Fear of what they are facing in this night world finally causes Emma to reach out for Bobby, but it is not until she overcomes her scorn of him in their real world that they are able to make contact in their dream life. When the terrifying climax to their shadow life comes, their concern for each other brings them through and cements the friendship that has been building.

THE MAGIC STONE. Illus. by John Kaufmann. New York: Harcourt, 1964. 223p.

The new housing project near Caroline's home has brought city people into the village. The children are tougher than Caroline and her brother Stephen, and seem unlike them in every way. But when Caroline and one of the project girls discover the magic stone, they learn it can bring understanding between them in spite of their differences.

SEA GULL. Illus. by Ian Ribbons. New York: Harcourt, 1966. 47p. o.p.
Stephen wants a parrot, one to sit on his shoulder as Long John Silver's did. When he finds the injured gull, he thinks that this would be better than a parrot. Granny will mend the gull, and then he can tame it and it will be his own. But Granny helps him to see, when the bird is healed, that a gull is meant to be wild and free.

THE SUMMER BIRDS. Illus. by James J. Spanfeller. New York: Harcourt, 1962. 155p.
Charlotte and Emma live with their grandfather and his housekeeper "in the turreted Victorian house called Aviary Hall, which name, as it turned out, was suitably prophetic." Each morning on their way to the village school, they wish that they might fly like the swallows they see skimming over the lawn. When the strange wild boy appears, their enchanted summer begins. First they and then their friends are taught to fly, and soon the boy is leading them as they soar and dive with the ease of birds. Only when they learn his secret do they realize how nearly they had followed their birdlike Pied Piper into his world. Only when they resist and he is gone do they realize what they lost.

WILLIAM AND MARY. New York: Atheneum, 1974. 160p.
Mary, whose father is the headmaster of a boarding school, and William, one of the pupils, are spending the holidays at the school with Mary's parents. Their first adventure occurs when William's half of a seashell is responsible for transporting them into a picture of Atlantis being swallowed by the sea. Mary begins to realize that William's strong desire to find the other half of his shell is the catalyst that projects them into fantastic underwater worlds. She does not understand William's anxiety, but in helping him she sorts out her own problems and comes to know his secret hope.

Retellings of Greek myths, in picture book format:

DAEDALUS AND ICARUS. Illus. by Chris Connor. New York: Harcourt, 1971. unp.

THE SERPENT'S TEETH: THE STORY OF CADMUS. Illus. by Chris Connor. New York: Harcourt, 1971. unp.

THE STORY OF PERSEPHONE. Illus. by Graham McCallum. New York: Morrow, 1973. unp.

Joyce Gard

Miss Gard was born in London in 1911, and when she was four, her parents moved the family to the country out of reach of the zeppelins. She found great joy in growing up in the country. Miss Gard says, "We were surrounded in childhood by wild flowers, birds, butterflies, and all the beauties of the countryside. These country things and the story books I lost myself in, hour after hour, whenever I had a chance, are my real biography. Beside them, the actions of my life are of far less interest."

She won a scholarship when she was twelve, and attended a girls' boarding school called Wycombe Abbey. Here, too, she lived in beautiful surroundings. Her favorite pastime was to climb a tree and sit in its branches to write poetry. She studied English language and literature at Lady Margaret Hall, Oxford. After she was graduated she worked for a year in the offices of Curtis Brown, the distinguished literary agent. She did a bit of teaching, too, but that was not satisfying.

The lure of Paris was irresistible, and she went there with high hopes of writing a book. Her associations with painters, sculptors, and writers, and her frequent visits to the art galleries and museums were an important part of her life there. She wrote one novel (unpublished) while in Paris, but when World War II came she returned to England to work in a war office. She experienced the blitz, as it was called, the bombing of London.

After the war she had intended to go back to writing again. But the death and the horror, the waste and destruction of the war

Joyce Gard. Photograph by John Webb, FRPS, London.

made her long to do something creative with her hands. So she took the necessary steps and became a potter. Making pottery was satisfying and she made good things, thanks to the potter with whom she worked in Winchcombe. A large collection of her wares was sent to New York on consignment one summer. But pottery leaves most of the mind free most of the time, and her mind was too active to be satisfied with that forever.

After nine years, she gave up the pottery and went back to London to write. Her first children's book was *Woorroo*, published in 1961. It had good reviews. When her third children's book, *Talargain*, was published in the United States, she was over-joyed.

"After that, my life became fairly uneventful, though more satisfying than it had ever been," she says. "If opening a kiln after a firing, in my pottery days, was exciting—and it never failed to give me a tremendous thrill—then having a book published was infinitely more exciting, giving me the sort of heady rapture which compensates for the long solitary hours of patient work, the days when the words will not flow, the wastepaper baskets full of discarded drafts, the unpublished manuscripts, and the lack of material security."

Now she lives in the beautiful countryside of Kent. "I have a cottage, a little green garden with three apple trees, good neighbors, a small car, a wood fire, and two adorable cats who keep me at work—for whatever happens, I must feed them and keep a roof over their heads.

"As for my writing, it is and will always be, the center of my life. I am never happy unless I have a book in hand—but I always have a book in hand."

Interview

Description is an outstanding part of Miss Gard's writing. Here she discusses why she feels it is so important.

It's a question of the necessity to make what I am writing as real as it can possibly be. In order to do this, I get into the skin of whomever I am writing about. I stand where they are standing, I look about me, and I write down as accurately as I can exactly what I can see and feel and smell. I think this is enormously important especially with anything that's slightly fantastic, because I think you have to have your feet hard on the ground in order to be able to make a fantasy credible. It's like Alice in Wonderland—when she wanted to come to this extraordinary world, she did it by falling down a rabbit hole, which is something very ordinary and the sort of thing anyone might do if he or she were small enough.

Miss Gard discusses the planning of her books before beginning to write.

I have the general outline of the story planned, but I never plan in detail because that would immediately kill the whole thing. I like to know roughly what's going to happen, but the details work themselves out as you go along. It's really like living a book, I have to live it. Otherwise, it means nothing at all.

In each of Miss Gard's books the setting is very important to the story. She discusses this in relation to one of her books.

The setting of *Smudge of the Fells* is of the greatest interest to me. I first began to be interested in the Lake District—where this book takes place—without really knowing that I was, because, when I was a little girl, we had the stories of Beatrix Potter. Before I could read at all, I was familiar with pictures which showed the countryside. Then when I first visited the Lake District, when I was a student at Oxford, it seemed like coming home. I thought it was wonderful. So, when I got to the stage where I wanted to write a children's book, I set it in the Lake District. I loved the area. The colors of the countryside are brighter there, the air is clear and very soft and gentle. It is really one of the places where I feel most happy and most at home any time of the year, but particularly in the spring when there are all these little lambs skipping around in a most frenzied way. As they play beside their mothers, they seem to wriggle all the way down their bodies to the very end of their tails. They gave me the idea for *Smudge of the Fells*.

I tried to write a book with London as the setting. I had a pottery at one time in a rather slummy part of London in which there were a great many coster-mongers that used to come around all the time. They're gypsies, really, but they call themselves general dealers. They go 'round collecting all sorts of refuse from people's houses that they can resell—old rags, old iron, old toys, anything that you don't want, that you throw out. They will give you perhaps a penny for it, but they really don't want to give you anything. They pretend they are doing you a great favor. They used to go along in front of the door all the time and I rather liked this, so, I thought I would write a book about it. I started to write a children's book about this neighborhood, but it didn't really come off because all the time I was longing to get to the country. I feel that if I were to settle in the country and never come near London, I would then be able to write about London.

TALARGAIN is a story of the supernatural, of a seal man in Northumberland. It is based on the idea found in many folktales and legends about the human-like qualities of seals, and the belief that humans may at times become seals, and seals may at times become humans. Is there a legend in Northumberland about a seal boy which gave you an idea for the story?

The legends of seal people come from throughout the whole of the British Isles, and I think, in fact, in all the countries where seals are frequently found. The Indians and the Eskimos have seal legends, and certainly the Norwegians and the Danes have them. Seals are very human in many ways. They have those wonderfully big eyes. They do look very human and they bob up at you out of the water, looking at you. They have a very funny way of crying almost like a child. I've been told that they love music, and when music is played they will come up out of the sea and listen, although I've not actually experienced that. Particularly in all the Celtic lands of Britain (for the whole of Britain was Celtic before the peoples came from the Continent), there were seal legends, and there still are seal stories in all the Scottish islands and highlands.

There's a book called *The People of the Sea* by David Thompson, which is a beautiful book, from which I got some of these seal stories that I used in my book. The most important source for *Talargain* was a ballad which I read a very long time ago when I was a child, about a girl who was wooed by a seal man. It was in *The Child's Book of Ballads*, which is a wonderful collection.

Is there some feeling that still persists in Northumberland about seals communicating with people?

All through the Northern Isles the belief still persists that seals are people and that sometimes people are seals, because there are very strange stories about women, for example. Somebody will say, "Have you ever seen Mrs. So-and-So except in a very long dress? That's because she hasn't got legs, because she's a seal lady, really." I don't know if it still goes on quite like that, but there is certainly a very strong feeling that seals when swimming can become human, and humans when swimming can become seals. They also believe that seals are the spirits of drowned sailors.

There were two reasons, one personal, why I chose to present Talargain's story through present-day Lucilla. It was partly that I wanted to frame the story. It's like a picture seen through a frame, and the frame is modern day—this modern-day girl looking through this picture. And it was partly because my mother came from the Northumberland coast. She used to tell me stories. They were the sort of stories that Lucilla's mother used to tell her. Stories about wonderful picnics on the sands and how they used to go for moonlight walks. They used to find flowers along the rock tops. I think I put in that bit for her sake. Then, it was the first historical book I'd ever written, so, I couldn't write it directly. I had to do it through an intermediary who was Lucilla, a present-day girl. I thought it would make it more real.

There is a lapse of hundreds of years between Talargain's adventures and his meeting with Lucilla. Did he continue to exist throughout the time, or did he appear only when there was someone like Lucilla with whom he could communicate?

That's one of those things that I don't like to pin myself down to, too strongly. I think it is really up to the reader to make up his or her mind about that. I feel myself that he did only appear when there was someone he could communicate with such as Lucilla's old great-uncle (the old man in the shack), because he was the kind of person a seal would be able to talk to.

Will you tell us something about your most recent book, THE MERMAID'S DAUGHTER?

The Mermaid's Daughter has its setting in the Scilly Isles, which is a little group of islands off the southwest corner of England. They are very strange, mysterious islands with a great many very ancient tombs in them. It was my American publisher who first asked me to write about those islands. She had been there and she was enchanted with them. She said, "You must go to the Scilly Isles. You will find that the cats are all incredibly tame, and so are the birds, which is rather strange." I went there, and it is quite true. The birds are tamer than any birds that I have ever seen in my life. They hop down and talk to you almost as if they were like the seals—like spirits, like human spirits dressed as birds. And the cats are also very tame, too, in a funny way. They are different from any cats I've ever known. It's a very strange country. It is warm on account of the Gulf Stream, and you get tropical-looking lilies growing under the walls, and pretty-colored little succulents growing along the gray stone walls. It has got a special mystery and charm about it. And this story I wrote is about a girl who lived there during the Roman occupation.

Did you find the writing of any one of your books particularly difficult?

That's a funny thing. I never quite know about that. *Talargain* came very easily indeed, for some extraordinary reason. *Smudge of the Fells* was very difficult. I rewrote the first chapter about six or seven times, and yet everybody says that it reads very spontaneously. I just couldn't seem to get it out. I don't think it has anything to do with the book. I think it's something in the personal atmosphere around me, whether I can write easily or not. I don't know why. As for *The Snow Firing*, that wasn't very easy either. That is more realistic. Most of that happened to me, although, of course, the boy and the people are quite different. All the pottery bit I have included did actually happen to me because I went to work in a country pottery that was like the one I have written about.

I have to write. I'm not happy if I'm not writing. If it goes well, I enjoy it. There's nothing else I really care to do. It isn't always easy though. You have to get the word which says exactly what you want it to say, otherwise, there is no point in putting it down. I remember finding in Anthony Trollope's autobiography that I was reading not long ago, that he said that writing is not easy. His writing reads as though it was easy for him, but, of course, it wasn't.

Some Books by
JOYCE GARD

THE MERMAID'S DAUGHTER. New York: Holt, 1969. 319p.
> In a postscript the author gives evidence of a Sea Goddess cult centered in the Scilly Isles during the Roman occupation of Britain. Around this theme, she has woven a beautifully-written story of Astria, chosen in youth to be the symbolic mortal daughter of the Sea Goddess. It is a romantic tale of the joys and tragedies of Astria's life, and of the rites and beliefs of the island people as they relate to her—the Mermaid's Daughter.
>
> This is a long, complex novel for the mature reader.

SMUDGE OF THE FELLS. New York: Holt, 1965. 191p.
> A sensitive and moving story providing mystery and the details of present-day sheep farming in the Lake District of England. Fourteen-year-old Gerald Briggs can no longer stand to live in the same house with his devious and evil stepfather, Pim, who humiliates him at every turn. He seeks refuge in the cottage of old Lanty Jessup high in a remote area of the fells. When he finds Lanty in an unconscious state, he gives him aid and comfort, and in return, he is invited to stay. Gerald feels safe here, and with his constant companion, Smudge, a black lamb he rescued from its dead mother, he watches from afar the operations of the prosperous sheep farm, Greenrain.

But his watching soon draws him into a shocking episode which threatens his life and gives him a perspective about himself which he never had before.

THE SNOW FIRING. New York: Holt, 1967. 196p.

The setting is the Cotswold Hills in England. The plot revolves around the defunct pottery of Matthew Grange and the mystery that surrounds the old kiln that still remains on the property. Phillip Ruddock has grown up with no knowledge of the craft which meant so much to his grandfather. He always wonders why his mother refuses to talk about her father and the pottery, and forbids him to do anything with the old kiln or the pile of discarded pieces. Phillip admires young Claire and Rod Adamson who come to open the pottery, and with their help, he becomes devoted to the craft. The story moves quickly to a climax when a violent snow storm forces Phillip to do a "snow firing" alone, and some of the problems of the past seem to be resolved.

TALARGAIN. New York: Holt, 1964. 251p.

With its setting in the Farne Islands, the story is based on the folklore of the seal people, and the belief that humans are sometimes seals, and seals may become people. Talargain tells his strange and haunting tale to present-day Lucilla, revealing that he is a seal man with ancient background.

It is a mystical and beautiful story, skillfully told, with rich imagery of the Northumberland coast.

Alan Garner

Alan Garner grew up in the village of Alderley Edge in England and has seldom strayed far from his roots there. A childhood attack of meningitis kept him in bed for some time. During this period he lived with his grandmother, reading voraciously from her collection of Victorian books. In spite of this illness, he went on to become an outstanding athlete, winning several county championships at sprinting. He passed the examinations to enter Manchester Grammar School on a scholarship, and from there did his national service as a second lieutenant in the Royal Artillery. He began writing toward the end of his service. Another scholarship made it possible for him to attend Oxford, where he studied classical archaeology, which he confesses he found dull. Later, on his own, he discovered Celtic folklore and archaeology, and he found that these spoke to him in a way the classical did not. In 1957 he left Oxford and went home to try to become a writer.

Mr. Garner lives now with Griselda and his five children in an ancient house near Goostrey, not far from Alderley Edge. There he writes and pursues the study of archaeology, history, and folklore.

His house is itself an archaeological find. The present building dates from the fourteenth century, but the site has been occupied throughout the last four thousand years. It sits in a field at the end of a rutted track, well out of sight of the main road. Mr. Garner

Interview printed by permission of Harold Ober Associates, Inc. Copyright © 1976 by Alan Garner.

found the building neglected and dilapidated and moved into it though it had neither running water nor electricity. He is renovating the house bit by bit to make it comfortable, but he is intent on preserving its character. Among the finds he has made in and around the house are several wooden-soled leather shoes, the votive offerings which were built into the roof for good fortune.

From the window of his study he can see the enormous Jodrell Bank radio telescope moving almost imperceptibly in its tracking operation. Alan Garner finds it both right and pleasing that the old and the new should live side by side.

Interview

Three miles long and six hundred feet high, the hill called Alderley Edge rises abruptly from the Cheshire countryside. With its shadowy caves, its weirdly shaped rocks and dark woods, it is a place of enchantment for an imaginative child. As a boy, Alan Garner roamed freely here.

Today an inquisitive reader can explore the Edge and find on it the landmarks which Mr. Garner uses to root in reality Susan's and Colin's encounters with the Old Magic in THE WEIRDSTONE OF BRISINGAMEN *and* THE MOON OF GOMRATH. *From the Wizard Inn on the highway, a path slopes upward to the Edge and leads to the Golden Stone, an oblong rock of gray sandstone, its deep split mute evidence of the Morrigan's magical power. The sandy path widens to the left, rising gently under the shade of overhanging trees. The wood opens suddenly at the crest of the hill, revealing a broad stretch of bare stone and sand—Stormy Point, where Susan and Colin were attacked by the Svart creatures that came pouring out of the opening of the cave called the Devil's Grave. Nearby are the Iron Gates, the entrance to Fundindelve, where an ancient king and his knights lie in an enchanted sleep. Far below is the Cheshire plain, dotted with farms, and away to the right can be seen the moors and moun-*

Alderley Edge, the setting for several of Alan Garner's books.   Photograph by Cornelia Jones.

tains of the Pennines. On the other side of the Edge, where the forest thins a little and the sun dapples the floor, there can be seen the old straight track to the Beacon where Colin found the magic plant that saved Susan. Black holes mark the entrances to the tunnels and shafts of abandoned mines, both refuge and battleground for Svarts and dwarfs and other weird beings. Pine and fir and oak cover much of the hill. In the most thickly wooded areas, only a shadowy light comes through. The whole atmosphere is filled with primitive mystery and magic.

My first two books, *The Weirdstone of Brisingamen* and *The Moon of Gomrath*, are both set in the district around Alderley Edge in Cheshire, England. I set them there because it was the area I knew. My family had lived there for several hundred years, and I myself grew up there and ran wild all through my childhood on the hill called Alderley Edge. It's a very strange and mysterious place, and the atmosphere of it has always impressed me. So when I finally decided that what I wanted to do with my life was to write books, I turned to the thing which I knew best, which is what every writer does. In my case, it was Alderley Edge.

The books are fantasies, but they take place in a real setting, here and now. I think this is very important. It is for me, anyway—to write fantasy in a place where the reader can go and see and touch and experience for himself. If I were to make up these wild stories in a place of my own imagination, then somehow they would be cheating. It seems to me they would be cheating. This really stems from the frustration that I felt in my own childhood reading. Quite often when I'd read a book and been very impressed by it, I'd discover right on the last page that it was all a dream. We woke up. That seemed to me to be cheating. Or else the story would take place in some town called Ripchester or Moonville. Some of it didn't exist on the map and I could never go to it. But with my books, you *can* go. Every place that is mentioned *does* exist. My main reason for doing this is that I feel it makes the fantasy much more believable and stronger. For instance, on Alderley Edge there is a large stone called the Golden Stone. In *The Moon of Gomrath*, this stone is split by the Morrigan, who is a rather unpleasant witch. Now you may say to me, "I don't believe the Morrigan exists." But I can say to you, "Well, you go look at the Golden Stone. It's certainly split. Now, I don't know what split it, but I say it's the Morrigan."

Similarly, I use modern children and modern, ordinary, human characters in these stories. I do it to contrast with the wilder, more imaginative characters of folklore. It may or may not work. It's just the way that I find that I can do it. Some of the human characters, like the places, are real. Gowther Mossock, in *The Weirdstone of Brisingamen* and *The Moon of Gomrath*, was very much a real live farmer. He's dead now, but I've known him all my life.

In fact, I had to water him down slightly because he was much more colorful than I made him. So too with the Morrigan. She was somebody I disliked intensely.

> *A short way from the hill is the village of Alderley Edge, the setting for much of* ELIDOR. *The house to which the children return with the treasures from Elidor was Alan Garner's childhood home. A small, square, two-story brick house, it seems rather ordinary. Set low to the ground, with a door in the center, two windows above and two below and a chimney on each side, it has the look of the houses which small children draw. But this ordinary-appearing house becomes the scene of a terrifying attack by the forces of Elidor who have come to retrieve the treasures.*

The third book, *Elidor*, appears to be about somewhere completely different. It has nothing to do with the characters of the first two books at all, but it is still about Alderley Edge. Alderley Edge is both the hill with the strange wood that is the subject of the first two books and the village at the foot of this hill. It's in this village that I grew up. It's a modern village, suburban even, and it was this aspect of the Edge—of Alderley—that I used for *Elidor*. The cottage where Roland and his family go to live is the cottage where I grew up. The house, the road, the area—they're all exactly as described in the book. You can go there and touch it today, and again, the people are real people that I know.

But even in *Elidor*, which is set far more in the present, there is this mingling of modern children with characters based on folklore. You may say, "If they're real people that you use all the time, why do you need folklore? Why do you need its mysterious characters and these weird ideas?" I can't really answer that question because I don't know the answer. I think it's because in folklore, especially Celtic folklore—the stories of the people who lived here before the Romans came—are the people who speak most clearly to me. I understand their imagination. By taking these basic ideas from their legends, I can use that as a launching pad to get myself off the ground and my own ideas into orbit. I'm not saying it's a good thing to do at all. Other writers have other ways of writing, and I may myself grow out of this phase whereby I have to rely on a basis of folklore. But that's how it works for me. It may work differently for you. You see, you can't be taught how to write. The only way to learn is to go out and actually do it. That is, not to sit in a classroom and take notes, but to go out, take a piece of paper, and actually get down to the work of writing. To learn is to go out yourself and to do it.

Some Books by

ALAN GARNER

A CAVALCADE OF GOBLINS, edited by Alan Garner. Illus. by Krystyna Turska. New York: Walck, 1969. 227p.
> A collection of stories, both modern and traditional, from several countries.

ELIDOR. New York: Walck, 1965. 185p.
> While exploring a partially demolished church, Roland and his sister and brothers are spirited into the other world of Elidor. There they learn from King Malebron that the powers of darkness, led by the evil Vandwy, have ravished that once golden world. True to an ancient prophecy, the children recover the sword, the cauldron, the spear, and the stone which will restore the light to Elidor. When Vandwy attempts to regain the treasures, Malebron returns the children to their own world carrying the treasures for safekeeping. Secure in their everyday life, they begin to forget Elidor, until Vandwy sends his dark forces to break through to them.

THE MOON OF GOMRATH. New York: Walck, 1963. 184p.
> In this sequel to *The Weirdstone of Brisingamen*, the Morrigan again is spreading her evil over the land and has set out to destroy Susan. Colin and Cadellin and the elves fight to save her and themselves in a story even more gripping in its danger and enchantment than its predecessor.

THE OWL SERVICE. New York: Walck, 1967. 208p.
> An old Welsh legend tells of the love of two men for the same girl, and ends with the death of the men and the transformation of the

girl into an owl. In this modern-day story, set in a somber Welsh valley, we become aware that the pattern of the tragic triangle has been repeated several times through the centuries. Now it seems fated to recur, for Alison, her stepbrother Roger, and the Welsh boy Gwyn find themselves helplessly reenacting the legend in their own way and in their own time.

Awarded the Carnegie Medal, 1968.

THE WEIRDSTONE OF BRISINGAMEN. New York: Walck, 1960. 253p.

The legend of the sleeping king and his knights waiting to be summoned to save England in her greatest need forms the basis for the story of the missing weirdstone. When it is discovered that Susan's bracelet holds the lost stone, she and Colin are catapulted into the battle between good and evil for possession of the stone. The wizard Cadellin, protector of the king, and the Morrigan, a shape-shifting witch, lead the opposing forces. The struggle takes place on Alderley Edge and its environs, where present-day characters mingle with the strange creatures left from the days of the Old Magic.

Charles Keeping

Charles Keeping was born in 1924 in the London borough of Lambeth. A proud Cockney, he boasts one set of grandparents who were coster-mongers (street traders) and a father who was a professional boxer. He himself left school at 14 and was apprenticed in the printing trade. In World War II he served in the Royal Navy as a wireless operator. After the war he became a student at the Regent Street Polytechnic, working in drawing, etching, engraving, and lithography. His lithographs have been exhibited in several countries, and a number of museums and galleries own his work.

Since 1956 Mr. Keeping has illustrated a great many books by other authors and has written and illustrated picture books. His own city childhood has provided him with background for these original stories. One of them, *Charley, Charlotte and the Golden Canary*, was awarded the Kate Greenaway Medal in 1967.

With his wife and four children, Mr. Keeping lives in a rambling Victorian house on a tree-shaded street in south London. His large studio contains, in addition to his easel, comfortable chairs and a grand piano, suggesting that much of the life of the household is carried on in this room. At one end, tall windows look out into the garden. It is here that he works on his books and, more recently, on children's films for television.

Charles Keeping. Photograph courtesy of Oxford University Press.

Interview

I've illustrated books for children since I was five years of age. In fact, not for children, I've illustrated books and written story ideas for myself. Most of these ideas come really from my childhood when I lived in Lambeth, a part of London.

I was born in a house with a very small backyard. Because my father felt that children shouldn't play on the streets (it was a very poor area), I used to be put in this little yard at the back of the garden and I spent all my time in it. Next door to it was a stable yard where horses were kept for pulling carts, and somehow these things in this yard became very real to me. There was a fence, and over the fence was a big brick wall that was whitewashed. Everything seemed to happen in front of this fence. It was like looking at things on a stage. You saw people walk through the yard. They would lead a horse through the yard. There would be a dog in the yard. There would be chickens in the yard. I never spoke to any of these people because I was a little boy. I used to look through the cracks in the fence, so I was always looking at this isolated situation or image moving across. I started to create stories around these things so that the horse, the people, the chickens, the dogs, all became sort of symbols. Now, you understand what I mean by that? They became symbols of something rather than the things in themselves. I wouldn't say that I was sentimental about them in that sense. They just were symbolic.

You know, one learns so many things about life, but I think your clearest memories are the things that are most important to you. Later on you get somewhat intellectualized, so that you take a situation and you try to make it more clever than it really is. In those days one didn't. One just looked and one just used it.

Some people have said that cruelty has always had a strong part in a lot of my work. I don't think it's intentionally so. I first saw cruelty in that yard. We had horses, for example, and one day, say, a horse was by the fence and you could stroke it, and the next day it would be sold for dog meat. One couldn't understand this as a child, so these things became very real. You may have noticed this in my book, *Shaun and the Cart-Horse*. I gave it a happy ending, but the real ending wasn't very happy. The horse actually did go to be slaughtered. So these were things that were very real to one as a child.

But as I saw these things in this yard, I started to evolve stories around them. I think my sister actually joined me in this, and she used to write as well. We both grew up in this rather idyllic world of childhood, until my father died and we left that house. Certainly these early impressions were the strongest I experienced. They were so strong that I never thought of anything else than writing about them and drawing them.

I went to work at fourteen as an apprentice in the printing industry. My father died and my mother couldn't keep us both in school, so I had to leave and go out to work. Then along came the war and I ended up going into the Navy. I did four years in the Royal Navy, and after that I couldn't get a grant to become a full-time student. So I went to college as a part-time student and worked as a gas meter collector in North Paddington. You know, there was an awful lot that came out of that. I went in everybody's houses, saw the way people live. It was all in the poor parts of London, mostly in North Paddington and Kilburn and North Kensington, which is the poor area of Kensington and almost like ghettos. I never stopped drawing. Not until 1949 did I get a full-time grant to go to college. When I left, it was very difficult. To sell paintings was almost impossible. You could sell lithographs, but there was very little money in it. So I really started illustrating books right away. The first book I did was for people called Rathburn Books who, I believe, were American publishers, but I was sacked out of that. They thought my drawings were a bit way-out, and they said "No, thank you" after one book. But Oxford took me on in 1956, and since then I've illustrated steadily.

As I said before, horses are a symbolic thing. I'd always wanted to do something about a horse, but I've got an absolute dislike of humanizing animals. I can't bear animals to talk. I hope I'm not going to offend anybody by this, but I just can't stand animals to talk. I don't like railway engines that have got faces, either. I believe there's so much fantasy in real life that we don't need to do this. I know many people have done it successfully, but it's not a thing I would want to do. But I always wanted to use the real story of a horse. I did start on an idea, but I felt that I couldn't do this unless I'd got an actual animal in the actual environment that I was living in. So I first of all bought a donkey, which I said was for the children. This donkey was a vile little creature that bit and kicked. I had to sell it. A junk chap used to come around the streets, and he had an old black Welsh pony that was past its days. It was twenty years old, and it was due literally for the dog feed. I bought it off him, and slowly this idea evolved. In the original version of *Molly o' the Moors*, which was called *Black Dolly*, the horse died in the end. But the publishers felt that this was going just a little bit too far, so we had to give it a nice meadow. But I suppose that would be nearer the truth, really, because as you know, Black Dolly is outside these very walls now. She's in a little stable in the garden.

When I was writing *Charley, Charlotte and the Golden Canary*, I had a canary. I had it in a cage in that window there. I was getting towards the end of the book, and my aunt and uncle were staying with me at the time. My aunt contracted a disease of the eye while she was here and actually lost one eye. She loves canaries, so when the book was finished I gave her the golden canary and she still has it. It's very pleasurable for her now, because she can't see very well and she has this bird with her.

I've often been asked why I use such bright, vibrant colors. I don't always use bright colors, incidentally. Up to a while ago I used to work mostly in very sombre blacks and browns, and I think these bright colors came about for many reasons. One of them is, I think, that the city is full of brilliant color. This is not natural color, it is artificial color. You know, the whole tempo of the city is like—oh, like a jazz band, isn't it? It has this fantastic flashing-on of neon lights and things like this, and it has a sort of jarring quality of noise. Now we can't create noise. We can't have a book that makes a noise, so you see I often use color, again, in a symbolic way. I know that in America *Charley, Charlotte and the Golden Canary* was very much criticized for being almost over-brilliant in color. Many people thought, as one critic said, "It must have been a very dreary day in London, and Charles Keeping looks as though he got hold of his pot of paint and threw it in desperation at his drawing board." Well, you can tell them that isn't true. It was quite intellectually conceived. The color does have a jarring quality, I appreciate that. But this was done deliberately. I wanted to create almost a jarring effect on your nerves, so that you may experience some of the noise and the pulling down of old buildings and the building of new ones and all that general noise that goes on in a city. I think this is very much a part of it and was in my mind at the time.

In *Alfie Finds "The Other Side of the World"*, there again I was using amusement parks and things which are, in fact, a mass of neon lights. A child walking past them can one moment be green, the next moment red, and the next moment blue. In fact, he can be a part of all of these things at the same time. If you have a flashing-on neon light, he can have a red head and a blue body and green feet, you know, so I mean there's no reason why he can't be shown that way. Color is something I feel terribly strongly about because nobody is the same color for any one moment. The changing light of the day will change a person from one color to another. In a red setting sun a white horse will be pink. Next to snow, a white horse looks dirty yellow. I think people expect something to look the same color always, but it doesn't.

In the case of illustrating stories written by somebody else, it is often difficult unless you really like the story. I've illustrated things I didn't like. I'd better not mention any names. I can think of quite a few books I'd sooner not have illustrated. To do it well, I think that you must first of all take the story and really feel for that story, but not necessarily will it be the way the author himself felt about it. I mean it's quite likely that if I played you a piece of music now, you might see it just as a collection of intellectual sounds. Somebody else might see it as an evocative thing about the sea. You know, there could be all sorts of impressions one could get from listening to music and from reading words. So I would always illustrate a book according to how I feel about it and how I feel about the situation. It may not be always the way the writer felt about it.

I've been criticized once for this by somebody who said an illustrator (and I'll always give you the other side of the coin and help you to criticize me) should just be an accompanist to the writer. For instance, when you've got a singer, somebody plays the piano. I don't agree with that at all, really. I think if it works well—fine, it works well. But there is no reason why an illustrator couldn't do images that he himself feels are right but that would not necessarily please the author. He must be allowed to do it the way he thinks about it. He must be allowed, otherwise he is not an artist. If you are going to say an illustrator is just a satellite or an accompanist, well, you don't make much of him, and you rather reduce him, I think, by doing this. It means he's got to be a slave to the writer, and I don't approve of this at all. I don't think any writer would really want this. I think he would want the artist to make a contribution in his own right. This is what I would go out to do.

Certainly I would never illustrate a book, if I could possibly help it, in terms of the action or in terms of the kind of typical illustration we used to get. You know, where the story said, "Fred punched Bill in the nose." Then the illustrator drew it, and underneath the illustration was printed, "Fred punched Bill in the nose." This to me has never made sense. I can see no sense in illustrating something that's been written. I would much sooner do a drawing that created the mood of the chapter or the book or get something out of it as a mood thing. Even if it was a man hitting another man, then the real thing would be to create a violence, and that violence may be a part of that chapter. Therefore, the image itself should be a violent image. That's the first thing, not necessarily just a man hitting another man. This is what I feel very strongly about. I don't believe either that you should "steam-roll" over a book. That is, whether the book's a funny book or whether it's a serious book, the same old drawings get done. This again is wrong. You can't think about an opera, say by Mozart, the same way you feel about one by Verdi. And you'd use a different sort of singing. If you were singing in these operas, you would project your voice and your attitude in a different sort of way. I feel it is the same with illustrating. I'm not saying you should use a different style. This would be too conscious. I believe a natural difference will come out because you have got under the skin of that particular book and feel for that particular idea your way.

Let's make it quite clear on this question of illustration. I don't know that I've ever liked the word. In some way it seems to conjure up the idea of just making a point clear. I can't remember what the dictionary has to say, how it defines the word.

I think we ought to move towards making books as books.

I've only come close to it in *Alfie Finds "The Other Side of the World,"* but my next ones will bring this out more clearly. I think that what we've got to do is to look at a book as a physical thing in itself. Remember that it is a thing that you hold in your hand. It has two covers so far, though we may change that in the end. It has so many pages, and it has a time element. It's not like a painting. A painting you look at and you can normally see the total painting. A piece of sculpture you walk around. You can't just look at a piece of sculpture and say what you think about it. You've got to walk 'round it and examine it from all sides. A film—you have to go in and watch the film. You can't look at the still outside the cinema and say, "Now, that's a great film." You've not seen the film. It's no good going in and looking at the opening of the film and coming out. You've got to sit there and watch the whole film. It has a time element, and so has a book. Therefore, the book to me is very like a film, and my aim certainly is to create the type of book that is a total experience from the beginning to the end, in which the whole book is incorporated. In other words, the cover, the insides of the cover, the endpapers, the title page, the text—everything is a total whole, and it all works as a total thing. Also, it is a thing to hold in your hand and enjoy as a physical thing. You can get a book which may have been beautifully designed and beautifully thought out and yet has been badly reproduced and is a poor book. The book should be in itself a beautiful thing, and my aim is certainly to produce this.

I'm interested in television filming, and I believe we can make short, evocative films that are not necessarily preaching to anybody or not necessarily amusing anybody. The film is there as just a thing that, say, lasts for ten minutes, and you look at it and it evokes certain emotions, ideas, and feelings. I think we ought to do this in the children's book, too. I think the book ought to have a strong element of this, because I'm not out myself to entertain. Other people can probably do it much better than me. I'm out to produce something that is going to make a child look, enjoy, maybe think.

You know, I don't know how many people really get the point of *Charley, Charlotte and the Golden Canary*. If you look at it again, you'll find that both the girl and the bird were one and the

Charles Keeping's illustration that appears in color on the cover of *Charley, Charlotte, and the Golden Canary* (Oxford University Press, 1967; Franklin Watts, 1967).

same thing. They both were yellow and they both were behind bars. And in the end, all three of them were in a cage behind bars. I think it was the *New York Times* that said, "What a pity. It was such a trite little story." They were missing the whole point of the story. They got the impression that it was just a child who had lost his friend and then had found her through a bird. This was not the idea at all. The idea was to produce something which is very much a part of our life today. I started that story when I was walking 'round the Elephant and Castle [a district in London which got its name from a local pub] one day. I had a very good story about a canary which had been rejected by the publishers, and I was feeling a bit miserable. I walked 'round by the Elephant and I noticed these new big blocks of flats with all these very small children in the little balconies outside of the flats. You call them balconies, do you, with the iron grilles in front? The flats were so far up in the air that the mothers couldn't let their children come down and play, so they had to play on the balconies. Their whole lives were spent up there. This is true in London and I'm sure it's the same in New York. They just peer down like this, you know. But down in the street where the old houses were, there were all the normal little street herberts, as we call them, having some wonderful fights with dustbin lids and swords. And you could not look at the sparrows in the street and then at the canaries in their cages in the market there without making this equation between them. I wasn't trying to be a social reformer for children in that sense, but just to make something that comes out of a thought, out of an idea. I think any idea that comes to you like this is valid to children.

Alfie Finds "The Other Side of the World" was an interesting one, too, because I don't know whether anyone really ever got the point of that. Maybe I'm just bad at putting the point over. I remember a man one day telling his son what a wonderful footballer he had been as a young man. The father went on, telling all about his wonderful exploits and how he could have been quite a player. I suddenly thought how pathetic we all are in telling our stories. I knew this man, and I don't think he would ever have been a great football player. But he wanted to impress his son. Maybe he was dissatisfied with his life, his job. Who knows? My old man who talks to Alfie, you know, was the sort of old man who was just spinning the boy a yarn. Let's face it, he hadn't really been to the other side of the world at all. He only played outside a pub. I can't help feeling we're all basically liars. We're all basically fooling somebody or other. Yet children often not only want to be fooled, but they see things differently. I can remember as a boy how wonderful all those neon lights and things looked to me. They were like fairyland. Now I can go down to an amusement park and I can see that much of it is sordid and shoddy, and that there are fellows waiting to catch everyone. The kids go on the Dodgems and get cut short of their rides. But looking back in your own childhood, haven't you ever felt that we never saw it like that? Consequently, in *Alfie*, the reason I didn't draw amusement arcades, why it became just a blur of color, is because that's honestly how I feel Alfie would have seen it. I wasn't lying because the truth was there. I never said the old man hadn't been to the other side of the world, but the point was very few of these old boys had.

The next one, which is *Joseph's Yard*, involves a boy and a rose. It concerns this boy with the wanting to love something and who's jealous of it when he's got it. It also involves the boy's first realization that things die. It also has a happy ending. I don't know if life has a happy ending. I suppose it has, but you have to draw your own conclusions. Are you ever happy really with a beautiful thing? Does it always remain beautiful?

So you see my aims are to produce not another *Alfie*, not another *Charley*, but ideas as I see them and as they come to me. I don't think I ever set out to write a conscious story or ever will, but the thing is that the story evolves from ideas. If people want me just to write a story, some clever story that's going to please them, they'll have to look for someone else, because I just present them with ideas. And if they think the stories are trite, I can only say I'm sorry. That's the best I could think to do. It's exactly the same with the drawings, in that the drawings evoke just what I feel about something. I don't think this is so bad, because what are we all giving if not what we are? How boring it would be if we all gave the same thing.

Some Books by

CHARLES KEEPING

ALFIE FINDS "THE OTHER SIDE OF THE WORLD." New York: Watts, 1968. unp. o.p.

Old Bunty plays his gramophone outside the sugar factory and tells Alfie about strange, faraway lands. When Bunty disappears, Alfie crosses the river on the ferry and finds him and "the other side of the world."

CHARLEY, CHARLOTTE AND THE GOLDEN CANARY. New York: Watts, 1968. unp. o.p.

When Charlotte's house is torn down, she and her mother go to live in a new apartment building. Because the street is so far below their flat, Charlotte cannot go down alone. Lonely without her, her friend Charley buys a canary. When it flies away from him up to Charlotte's balcony, the two friends are reunited.

Awarded the Kate Greenaway Medal, 1967.

THE CHRISTMAS STORY. New York: Watts, 1968. unp.

The Nativity story.

JOSEPH'S YARD. New York: Watts, 1969. unp. o.p.

Living in the barrenness of a city slum, Joseph almost kills his rose plant with love, until he learns to share its beauty.

MOLLY O' THE MOORS. Cleveland: World, 1966. unp. o.p.

Molly tells the story of her life from show pony to junk dealer's cart horse. When she grows too old and worn to work, she goes back to live out her life in her old meadow.

THE NANNY GOAT AND THE FIERCE DOG. New York: Phillips, 1974. unp.

A little goat and her mother live in a weed patch near a junkyard which is guarded by a dog. On the morning after a night filled with bleating and barking, the mother goat is gone. The little nanny goat is terribly frightened but finally dares to go outside the fence. In a battle with the dog, she emerges the victor and knows she need never fear him again.

SHAUN AND THE CART-HORSE. New York: Watts, 1966. unp. o.p.
   When Uncle Charley Peel's cart horse is sold to the knacker, Shaun
   enlists the aid of his coster friends to buy her back.

THROUGH THE WINDOW. New York: Watts, 1970. unp. 100p.
   All that Jacob knows of the world is the part of the street he sees
   through the window. There is the church, the sweet shop, the brewery, the old woman and her dog. When the runaway brewery horses
   kill the old woman's dog, Jacob breathes on the window and draws
   his own happier ending to the story.

Allan Campbell McLean

Allan Campbell McLean was born in an industrial city in northern England, the youngest of a family of eight. At an early age he was determined to write, but it was difficult to get a start. However, before he left school at the age of fifteen, he had written his first story.

His first job was as an apprentice motor mechanic, but he soon found that unsatisfactory. Later he worked as an office boy with a firm in Barrows-in-Furness.

When he was eighteen he joined the Royal Air Force and saw service in the North African and European theaters. During World War II he married, and at the close of the war he and his wife lived in County Kent, south of London.

He immediately began work on his first novel, but their money was running low. They needed a less expensive place to live, away from the bustle of the metropolitan area, where he would have more solitude for his writing. The Isle of Skye seemed to fit his need, and shortly after their first child was born, they moved into a tiny croft on Skye.

Life was difficult for the first few years. There was a new mode of living to be learned. Here life was dependent on the land. There are few trees on Skye, and no coal. The residents cut their own peat for the fireplace, their only source of heat. Fortunately for the McLeans, their neighbors were helpful, and life on Skye became more and more appealing. Then, as his reputation as a writer grew and he began to have his books published, they were able to move into a larger and more adequate house.

Their three children were raised on Skye. They all have the beautiful, melodic speech of the Islanders that shows the influence of the Gaelic tongue and is quite different from their parents' British accent.

The children are all grown now, and Mr. and Mrs. McLean have moved to the mainland of Scotland. They live in Inverness where he continues to devote his full time to writing.

Interview

I was an age of twenty-five before I went to Skye, and I was intrigued by the island, by these immense stretches of hill and sea, wonderful country. Above all, I was enormously impressed by the people, because I had been brought up in an industrial town in England, a shipbuilding town. For the first time in my life I encountered what I suppose one must call a peasant community. English was not their mother tongue. The mother tongue, the tongue they used in everyday life, was Gaelic, and the English they spoke had a sort of Biblical simplicity. I was so impressed by the characters I encountered there, by the island itself, by the whole concept and way of life that was different from anything I had known before, that I determined to attempt to get this down on paper.

Mr. McLean's daughter, Catriona, commented on her life as a child growing up on a croft on the Isle of Skye.

Well, at the time it was just our way of life, and it seemed in no way out of the ordinary. But looking back on it, I see we had greater advantages than the children in town. When the little children first started to school, in fact, we felt a little out of place because most of the children in the first class couldn't speak English at all. They only spoke Gaelic, but we and the teachers gradually taught them to speak English. We lived off the main road, and we stepped out of the house into the fields, and there were hills behind us. We made our own amusements because there was none of the kind of entertainment one finds in town. We would help with the hay, with the cutting of the peats, and sometimes we would go over the hill in the back of the house to the shore. There was a lovely sort of secluded beach in the back there. The Festival of Gaelic Music was held once a year, and all the outlying schools met at Portree, the capital of Skye, to compete in this festival. This annual Mod was really the high spot of our lives when we went to school.

Mr. McLean continues to discuss his writing.

I was never really terribly interested in writing books for children, if I must be honest. Like all young writers, when I first started, I was going to write the great novel of the year. I gradually became aware, with a little more age and possibly a little more wisdom, that I wasn't competent to do this and I thought, mistakenly I believe now, that it would be easier and more within my competence to write a children's book than to write another novel. I hope this may be of some benefit to any aspiring writers who are listening to me. I then sat down and wrote *The Hill of the Red Fox*. I had almost finished it when I said to myself, "What am I doing writing this? Nobody will read it. Put it away." Months and months later I took out the manuscript and finished it, not with any real conviction. Now as it happened, it was extremely successful. As I wrote it originally the villains were not Russians. They were, in fact, Germans. They were a group of Nazis who had settled in the Argentine and hoped from a base there to build up their strength. I didn't select Russians as villains because I thought it was much too conventional to have Russian villains and that perhaps in later years, if the book were still being read, it might well be that there would be a greater degree of realism in having some ex-Nazis as the villains. Unfortunately, I allowed myself to be talked out of this by my publishers. But I'm glad to say that ever since that day, I have never been talked out of anything. I have been very fortunate in that respect. I have not had as much as a word altered by suggestion in any other book that I've ever written.

Now I don't believe myself that *Hill of the Red Fox* is a particularly good book. I think it was well received by critics here and in the United States, but in my opinion the plot is a purely mechanical one. I take the view that it isn't necessary to look for Russian villains or German villains. I think what is much more interesting than having purely mechanical plots is to look a little more deeply into one's own social history and one's own country. There are plenty of heroes and villains to be found there. There is a great deal of drama, there is a great deal of color in what seem to be fairly mundane events in the normal work that people do. I think it is much more interesting to look at this—to try to discover why people acted as they did, how they acted at a particular time —and consequently to concentrate much more in attempting to depict a certain society at a certain time, and the people within that society.

The period in which *The Ribbon of Fire* and *Sound of Trumpets* were set—the 1880s—was a time in which I think the young people in America should be particularly interested. This was a period when crofters in the highlands of Scotland were greatly oppressed by the land owners. In consequence of that oppression, it became much more profitable to have sheep in the glens than human beings, and the shortsighted landlords, who were concerned with personal profits, cleared people from the glens and substituted sheep in their place. These stupid and essentially vicious landlords were not aware of the great damage they were doing in their own country. Surely one can see how shortsighted such a view was, when human beings who were considered of such little account crossed the Atlantic in floating coffins (many died on the way), and survived to make an immense contribution to the building of your own country. Indeed, the conditions of life that are enjoyed by the young people in America today are due in great measure to the work of immigrants, not only immigrants from the Scottish Highlands, of course, but from throughout Europe. Those young people in America who bear Scottish names, whose forebears came from Scotland, should be aware of this period of history. Looking at it over a period of time, one can see that Scotland's loss was purely America's gain.

Now, if you are writing an adventure story, it is, of course, essential to know the end of the story before you begin to write.

However, the beginning is the most important part of the story, in my view, and it is the most difficult because you have only that terrible blank sheet of paper before you. You have nothing to build on. This is terribly difficult. I try to know the beginning, and I try to know the end, and usually in some miraculous fashion the rest emerges and develops as I write.

Mr. McLean discusses some of his ideas about character development, and why he writes in first person.

Every writer probably bases his characters to some extent upon people he has known, although the outcome often surprises him. The author could start out with a quite safe sort of character who might well change into a fairly desperate villain. Yes, I think certain of my characters are based on people I've known. Character Worley, a swashbuckling character who figures in some of my children's books, is based in part upon a man I knew who really should have been born in an earlier age, perhaps should have sailed with Captain Morgan. It's terribly difficult to attribute just how much goes into a character from people one has known in his life —a sort of composite, I would imagine.

I think I write in first person in order to create a greater credibility, so that the reader becomes involved and can identify more easily and sympathize more readily when he sees the whole action of the story and all the reactions to events in the story through the eyes of one particular character. Writing in first person creates terrible technical difficulties because the author has got to see every aspect of the story through one pair of eyes. Sustaining tension in a narrative to the very end is troublesome because you cannot change the scene so easily when one person is telling the story.

I can't really say that I have a favorite character; it is difficult to answer that. In one of my early books there was an old crofter— I've forgotten his name now—who related to the boy in the story. He'd been a great traveler—the old man—and talked about the great fighters he'd seen—the boxers and prizefighters. I remember he told the boy about Jack Johnson, who used to walk a tiger or a lion around on a leash. I had great sympathy for that old man, so possibly he was one of my favorite characters.

I've been toiling for a considerable time on a new children's book. I didn't want to go on just writing adventure stories. Neither did I simply want to write historical novels. I'm now going back to a period in 1877, but I hope this book will be a little different from any other. Essentially, it's concerned with a Christ figure, and it tells a story of intolerance, of the essential inhumanity of men to men through the eyes of a young boy. I hope it will have a great deal of relevance, not only to young people in this country, but equally to young people in the United States. It's a difficult book, but I hope eventually to get it done before I am clapped into a debtor's jail.

Some Books by
ALLAN CAMPBELL McLEAN

MASTER OF MORGANA. New York: Harcourt, 1959. 222p. o.p.

The ruggedly beautiful Isle of Skye is the background for this fast-paced, far-above-average adventure mystery of salmon poaching. Niall's brother Ruari, one of a crew of salmon fishermen, has chosen for some time to spend his weekends at the fishing station even though the boats do not go out. When Ruari is brought home on a stretcher, battered and unconscious, Niall suspects that it is not an accident. When pages of his brother's diary are stolen by a stranger posing as an insurance man, Niall is convinced. Replacing Ruari in the fishing crew, Niall secretly begins to explore the possible causes of his brother's injury. Although his own life is also threatened, Niall finally discovers the meaning of Morgana and the mastermind of its operation.

STORM OVER SKYE. Illus. by Shirley Hughes. New York: Harcourt 1956. 256p.

A remarkable and exciting story of sheep smuggling in a small village on the Isle of Skye. The usual trust that exists among the sheep owners is broken in November by the loss of sheep from each flock, and the men realize that one among them must be a thief. The suspicion grows through the winter and spring, destroying the peace of the village, until a frightening incident brings it all to a head, and the story moves swiftly to a dramatic climax.

The literary quality is outstanding, the characters are strong and well drawn, and the wild and beautiful Isle of Skye is vividly described.

RIBBON OF FIRE. New York: Harcourt, 1962. 191p. o.p.

A SOUND OF TRUMPETS. New York: Harcourt, 1966. 192p. o.p.
For generations the crofters on the Isle of Skye have struggled endlessly to make their living along the craggy coasts, on the lonely moors, and in the rugged mountains. In the 1880s their homes and properties are threatened by the encroachment of the absentee landlords, the Lairds.

In these two historical novels, the author has written stirring accounts of the struggle of these proud and strong-willed people to keep their independence. They are powerful and suspense-filled stories distinguished by superb writing.

THE YEAR OF THE STRANGER. New York: Walck, 1972. 192p.
1877, the year of a disastrous flood on the Isle of Skye, is the period setting for this moving historical novel. The story is told by Calum Og, a volatile and courageous lad whose father became an outlaw when some farming families were evicted from their homes and driven to the rocky shores. Calum attempts to aid Mata, the tinker, who has once befriended him, but who has now been caught for salmon poaching and is driven from the town during a fierce storm. A stranger brings calm to the ensuing conflict, and in the weeks that follow, crops thrive and the herring are plentiful. But the torrents of rain and the flooding return when the stranger, attempting to share the harvest with the poor, is driven from the town. Calum later has glimpses of the stranger in a hidden glen where life is transformed for those who live there.

Margaret MacPherson

Margaret MacPherson's childhood summers were spent at her father's birthplace on the Isle of Skye. She remembers with joy playing on the hills, catching the ponies that roamed free in the summer and sometimes riding one of them bareback. In the winters she went to school in Edinburgh.

Mrs. MacPherson later took a Master of Arts degree from Edinburgh University. She graduated in the morning and was married in the afternoon. Her husband was a cattle and sheep dealer whose home was on Skye.

When the hard times of the Depression came, she and her husband rented a peninsula of five thousand acres from the Forestry Commission and began to graze cattle and build a sheep stock. It was a remote place, accessible only by boat; the nearest house was two-and-one-half miles away. Their house, she says, was too hot in summer, too cold in winter, and rocked like a cradle in the wind. But it was a happy place for her husband and herself and their sons. They lived there for ten years until World War II, when help became hard to get. It was then they took a croft near the town of Portree on Skye.

Mrs. MacPherson had many interests other than the croft. She was a Member of the Commission on Crofting and was active in politics. When her seven sons were older, she took a Teacher's Training Course in Edinburgh and for a time taught school on Skye. She wrote articles and talks for the British Broadcasting Corporation. As her sons grew up and scattered, she found that she "had about two spare hours in the afternoon" and began to write a book. She has been writing ever since.

Two of her sons work the place on the peninsula where she and her husband began crofting. Another son works the croft near Portree. She herself has a bungalow on that croft, and her grandchildren running in and out keep her lively.

Interview

Margaret MacPherson and her husband brought up their seven sons on a croft on the Isle of Skye, off the coast of Scotland. It is this island, where she still lives, that is the setting for all of her books.

This Isle of Skye is a very famous one, I think, because it's so beautiful. It has very high, rugged hills and some of the best climbing in the British Isles, and it has a very variegated coastline. You get high cliffs and you get rocks and you get little sandy places—but not much sand. It's mostly rock, so that you can learn to climb rocks right from the start. It's all cut up into crofts. A croft is like a small farm. Children on these crofts all play together, of course. They work together, too, because children on a croft usually have quite a lot to do.

My sons grew up in a very wild place, not the place we're in just now but over behind the Cuillin Hills. We had no road and were seven miles from the nearest shop, but we had the sea at our doors. The boys, as soon as they could stagger, were out after cattle or they were out to snare rabbits or they were out to work the sheep in the fanks [where the sheep are sheared] with their father. They adored doing that. When they weren't doing it in the summer, they were doing it in pretense in the winter, driving each other into pens and shearing each other on the kitchen floor. They had the greatest fun. Then we used to go round the shores—what do you call it, beachcombing—and get all kinds of wood and stuff that came across the Atlantic, perhaps, or from ships that had broken up. There was an awful lot of it in the wartime because the ships were being blown up by the Germans, and we used to get all kinds of things on the shores. We had a boat, too, and we used to go round the cliffs at night fishing for cuddy. We would put out a net for salmon. There were deer on the hill. Of course, there were also the cattle to look after and hay to secure. Then the boys all learned to milk. So, really, there was a great deal to do. Oh, dear, there was never a dull moment.

I've never put one of my own boys as a character in a book. I don't think you do that, but you take bits of people and mix them up together in your own mind. Then they go into your books. Of course, I've used the boys because they played shinty. Now shinty is a Highland game. It's not really like hockey. It's a much faster game with a lighter club which is used above the head, and the players have to have a very good eye for hitting in the air. The ball will go from one end of the shinty pitch to the other very quickly. All the boys adored shinty. I think their father influenced them in that. When they were small, I had every window in my house broken with shinty balls going through them. It was very annoying in wartime because you couldn't get glass to replace. We had these boxes nailed over the windows and, my word, they didn't keep the cold out very well. So we used to get rather annoyed about that. Then they had a place on the croft which we called the shinty pitch. Every winter evening after school, they played shinty there until it was so dark they could hardly see the ball. And they played in spring and summer, too. This was *the* game. Many a time I've stood watching shinty matches, blue with cold, because they usually played in winter. But they managed to enjoy it. The only sad thing is that shinty has died out in Portree now, but it is very much a game in Scotland still, and a very good one.

I have no character in mind when I begin to write a book—none at all. When I put characters on paper, heaven knows what's going to come out of them. That rather makes the fun of writing for me. I start off with a character and think, "Oh, well, he'll do this and he'll do that." But will he, when he gets his own way? Not a bit of it. He says, "No, I'm not going to do that and I won't do this and I'll do something else, and that's for you."

For instance, Jim in *The Rough Road*—now, I didn't know what to make of him. He was a very—well, not a very lovable boy, and yet there was something nice about him. As he went on and as he became fond of the drover and as he became fond of working, he developed all kinds of strength in his character which I didn't think he had to begin with. He turned out a lot better than I had thought in the first place. And also, the boy in *Ponies for Hire*. He was a milksop, if you like. Oh, he was a very tiresome character, pretending to be grown up beyond his years, as some people do when they are really making up for being rather weak in body. Then when he grew up, he got fond of riding ponies and running the pony farm. He grew quite decent, really, and I became quite fond of him in the end, although I hadn't much time for him in the beginning. So that's how it goes, you see. They live and they produce their own characteristics as you go along.

I have two favorite characters, one a boy and one a girl. I really became very fond of Jim. He was the orphan who had such a terribly bad time in *The Rough Road*, and I think he stuck it out pretty well. The other favorite character I have is in *The New Tenants*. This was a girl from Glasgow. When she came up to Skye, she had to cope with a class of boys who all thought they didn't want a girl among them and, especially, they didn't want a girl from Glasgow. They were rather nasty to her, as boys can be sometimes, until at last they became friends. She still got through it very well, and I liked her because she was firm and was also brave without making a great deal of fuss about it.

Nothing inspires me at all when I begin to write. I sit down and there's the paper. Oh, heaven, what a grind it is until you get underway. I do have the germ of an idea or the gist of an idea. For instance, the first book I ever wrote was about smugglers. The people I sent it to said, "Oh, no, this is very old hat; everybody writes about smugglers. You must try and find something original." So I said, "What the dickens is original about this place?" Then I thought, "Oh, shinty, dash it all, of course shinty is original." Then that was the gist of the idea, but that was all I had, so I wrote SHINTY at the top of the page and then off we started. But I hadn't a notion how to work it out except just the idea of boys trying to keep a shinty team together when it was going to be stopped. This was how *The Shinty Boys* began. In *Ponies for Hire*, all I knew was that the girl was going to lose her pony and, therefore, how was she going to keep it? In *The New Tenants*, the idea was of people coming up from the south and not knowing anything about crofting, and having to make a go of it somehow or other, and being very poor and making all kinds of mistakes. Apart from that I didn't know anything about the characters I was going to write about, and they just grew. Oh, how I wish I was inspired. How nice it would be!

Some Books by
MARGARET MACPHERSON

THE NEW TENANTS. Illus. by Shirley Hughes. New York: Harcourt, 1968. 254p. o.p.

> When old Uncle Fergus dies, Liz and her family come from Glasgow to Skye to farm the croft. They are city folk, ignorant about farming, and Dad is thankful for Danny Ross's help. Liz soon begins to realize that Danny is not as helpful as he seems and is purposely leading them astray. But Dad trusts him and is furious with Liz when she tells him of her suspicions. Her friendship with neighboring Hamish Macdonald leads her to prove Danny's treachery and assure their staying on the croft.

PONIES FOR HIRE. Illus. by Robert Parker. New York: Harcourt, 1967. 191p.

> Kirsty's brother Roddy, the man of the family since their father's death, is determined to get a tractor or give up the farm work and go to sea. Taking tourists in to board seems a possibility for making money, and the whole family gets busy preparing the house. When the first tourists arrive, Kirsty and her brothers are disappointed to find that they are a mother and her sickly, snobbish son. Much to Kirsty's surprise, she and Nick become friends. It is Nick who dreams up the pony-riding plan which eventually brings in enough to make the tractor a reality.

THE ROUGH ROAD. Illus. by Douglas Hall. New York: Harcourt, 1965. 223p.

> Jim lives with Sarah and Donald Bruce, the dour, hard-bitten foster parents who underfeed and mistreat him. When Alasdair MacAskill comes to Brae and allows him to help with the cattle, Jim gives him the love and respect which his parents have not warranted. When

MacAskill is injured and Jim takes charge of his cattle at the big
Dingwall sale, it precipitates a fight between Jim and the Bruces.
Because MacAskill then turns against him, Jim is filled with resent-
ment until he learns that MacAskill, in his own way, cares for him.

THE SHINTY BOYS. Illus. by Shirley Hughes, New York: Harcourt,
1963. 224p. o.p.

Shinty has to be given up, the schoolmaster says. Equipment is expensive and there is just no money for it. But Neil and his friends
are determined to save the game they love. Yet how in the world can
they make money when they work all summer on their fathers'
farms? They find ways: helping tourists, running errands, saving
gifts from aunts and uncles, and winning prize money at the Highland Games. Even the visiting girl cousin whom Neil is prepared
to dislike is a help. When summer is over and they still are short,
help comes from a most unexpected source. Shinty is saved!

Kathleen Peyton

Kathleen Peyton has been writing and sending manuscripts to publishers since she was nine years old. Her first book was published when she was fifteen and was studying at the Manchester School of Art. After finishing her course at the art school she was married, and she and her husband spent a year working their way across Europe. Later they worked and traveled in Canada and returned home by way of the United States. They now have two daughters.

Mrs. Peyton and her husband chose K. M. Peyton as their pseudonym at the beginning of their careers, but *Sea Fever* is the last book they worked on together. He is an artist and photographer.

Sailing is an abiding interest. She and her husband owned a Dutch fishing boat until it proved too big to maintain. They now own an eleven-ton, thirty-year-old Norwegian-built gaff cutter in which they sail the waters of the North Sea.

When not sailing or writing, Mrs. Peyton enjoys music, walking, and gardening.

Kathleen Peyton. Photograph by Michael Peyton.

Interview

I didn't really start to write just by saying that I was going to write a book. When I was small, I was always writing. I think I was nine when I started my first story which was long enough to call a book. It was all written in longhand, of course, and was called, I remember, *Gray Star, the Story of a Race Horse*. It was in the first person. *I* was the race horse. After that I always had a book going. They used to come out so that they were full-length, quite long books. As soon as I finished one, I started another. Once when I was at school, a teacher asked me to do some illustrations for a book. I said I'd do the illustrations for my own book. She was interested, so she read it. She thought it was good and told me to get it typed. I sent it to a publisher, and it was accepted for publication when I was fifteen.

Kathleen Peyton has placed her stories in the same setting in which she herself has lived. This is in the eastern part of England in the county of Essex, near where the Thames and the Crouch and the Blackwater flow into the North Sea. Nearby at Burnham on the River Crouch are the saltings, the grassy areas that are covered when the tide comes in. As on much of the Essex coast, a sea wall helps control the water. But even so, there are two houses here which are flooded when the tide is very high. They have plugs in their floors which are pulled to drain out the water. These houses were what she had in mind, Mrs. Peyton says, for the house of the boy in THUNDER IN THE SKY. *Inland is the rolling countryside that was the setting for* FLAMBARDS, *as well as the little run-down thatched farmhouse used for* FLY-BY-NIGHT. *The land is fairly flat but there are hills around, some of the hills high enough so that from them the River Crouch can be seen in the distance. On the north bank of the Thames are the Maplin Sands, which make the mouth of the Thames so dangerous and which gave* THE MAPLIN BIRD *its name. Farther north on the River Blackwater is Maldon, where the huge sailing barges are moored.*

There are still quite a lot of fishing boats working from the area, and a few of the barges that used to do all of the trading in the old days are still sailing around here. Most of the barges are at least eighty feet. They vary from eighty feet long to one hundred feet. But they are so cleverly designed that two people can manage them, although it can be very, very hard work. There's still one sailing barge now trading, just one. It hasn't got an engine and it's skippered by an old boy called Bob Roberts. You see him still around here. He brings the barge up the Crouch sometimes or up to Maldon or up to London quite a lot, and he's carrying cargo without an engine. He's the only one left now.

I was interested in barge sailing because you see so much of it around here. When we go sailing, we see these barges sailing in the same waters. They're so picturesque, you can't help but stop and look at them. Most of them still haven't got any engines, and they sail under a huge mainsail and a foresail and a mizzen at the back. They do these fantastic passages, and when the wind blows up they really go very fast. We go and watch when they have a race. There are three races every summer—one on the Thames, one on the Medway, and one up here on the Blackwater. We generally take our boat and sail along with the race. If the weather blows up, it's a wonderful sight to see about twelve barges all racing, sailing as hard as they can go.

I think every book I've written so far, with perhaps the exception of the one about flying, is definitely written through things I've done. In *The Plan for Birdsmarsh*, for example, where they're testing out that rubber suit, the lifesaving suit that the boy wants to develop—that is all absolutely true. A friend of ours invented this suit and we used to test it for him from our own boat in the middle of winter. He actually swam across the Channel to France in it and came back without any escort boat at all. When he got back to England, he couldn't get in to the shore. The tide kept sweeping him out, and he went up on the Goodwin Sands and took refuge on one of these buoys until the tide turned and he could swim in. The funny part was that after all he'd been through crossing the Channel, he got terribly seasick sitting on that buoy.

I've sailed all that area that comes into the sailing stories. My own experiences definitely went into *Sea Fever* and *The Maplin Bird*. When Emily is frightened on a boat in *The Maplin Bird*, it's very much how I felt a couple of times. We have had some very bad experiences. My husband learned to sail just by sailing. He didn't know how to sail, but we bought a boat and just went off. We had the children with us on one occasion when they were very small, just three and four. We were in the Thames estuary, and we had some rigging failure and the engine wasn't working. We had to run before the winds out of the estuary and there was very rough weather. We had to do what we could. We got out off Harwich, which is quite some way out, and we thought we would be able to point into Harwich, but it happened we couldn't. The wind came around and we were going straight out. It was dark, by this time it was midnight, and I was very worried about the children. In the end we flashed up a ship and a steamer came up and took us off. It was pitch dark and very rough, and it was really quite a frightening experience. But it was very useful afterwards knowing how people feel.

I bought a pony that was unbroken and very much like Fly-by-Night in character. He was a very cocky little pony, not a bit docile. My poor daughter did all the suffering just like Ruth in the book. Of course, the circumstances aren't exactly the same. We didn't have Ruth's money problems exactly, but all the actual experiences with the pony were very much what happened to us. My daughter was frightfully keen to get her pony jumping and going around the course in the hunter trials, which she did in the end. She came third in the trials, which is even better than Ruth did.

Everything in the background of *Sea Fever* is absolutely authentic, the way these old fishermen lived. In *Thunder in the Sky*, the actual plot of the spying I made up, although it was going on all the time during the war. But all the part of the barges going across the Channel and how the war affected them is perfectly authentic. There are a lot of these barges moored up at Maldon, which is near where I live, and I have been on board them. I have been all around, and we know quite a lot of the skippers, and we have sailed on them ourselves. But I also had to do an awful lot of research for that because the technical side of it is very difficult, and I had to have quite a lot of help with it. I wanted it to read so that anyone who had sailed a barge would read it and not say, "That's wrong. That's wrong. That's wrong." I was very careful about that. I don't think there are too many inaccuracies in it.

The characters in *The Edge of the Cloud* are fictional, but all that about the way the early flying took place and the adventures they had in flying the Channel is as authentic as I could make it.

I think that getting help from other people is very necessary because you can't know all these points that arise. For example, I needed medical advice in *Flambards* for the problem of Will breaking his leg. I wanted him to be injured in such a way that he would be fairly active for other things but would not actually be able to ride a horse again. It was very difficult to work something out which would just cover this point, but I did manage it with some medical advice. Then I had some more trouble afterwards when I wanted to write a sequel. It was necessary then that William should be able to fly an airplane, which wasn't easy when he had a stiff leg. I had to have medical advice to see how this leg could be fixed again, which at that period apparently was not a very easy thing to do. But I was assured it was all right, that it could be done in Switzerland. This dictated a part of the plot, really, because it meant he had to go to Switzerland.

I know fairly well what's going to happen when I start a book. I always know the theme, obviously, and what the whole point of the book is, what the main story line is, where I want to finish. Generally I know that, but sometimes I'm not always clear about how I'm going to develop the middle. Naturally you have to know what you're going to write in the beginning, and I always have the end fairly sure in my head, but sometimes the middle is a little loose. But I always find as I go along that it all falls into place. Not just like that, it doesn't just happen. Obviously it doesn't just happen. Sometimes I have to sit and pray hard about it. I find that sitting on a train I get very good ideas. I don't know why. My husband always thinks his ideas up in the bath. I find that going up to London on the train, which takes fifty minutes, is very productive. If I have a bad problem, I always think, "Oh, I'll work that one out on the train." It seems to work.

I don't start a book saying that I want to develop this character in this particular way. I don't think I'm conscious of it really, but I realize myself that the interest to me in writing books is always in the characters of the people. I find that I use the plots to follow my own interest in the people, so to speak, and I find that the plots grow from the way the people interact one on the other. I don't sit down and write a book and say this is going to be about the growth of this character. But I've heard this said so often about my writings. It must be something about the way I work, the way I like to make out my plots.

My characters are never anybody I know very well. I sometimes start off on a character perhaps by using somebody I've met once. Winnington, in *The Plan for Birdsmarsh*, was somebody I met on vacation, and I used him. Of course, I didn't really know him. It was only his appearance, really, and his superficial character that came over to me that I used. For example, the character I'm writing about here now is a boy I've seen but have never spoken to. I just thought that that's the type I wanted to write about, just from his looks, but I shall never meet him again. That sort of starts you off. I think my female characters always seem to come out the same, which isn't very satisfactory. Emily in *The Maplin Bird* and Christina in *Flambards* are rather the same character, which annoys me a bit. But on the whole, I don't think I base my characters on real people.

I don't really have a favorite among my books. I always like the one I'm writing now better than any of the others. Once they are written, I sort of forget about them, really.

> *Her readers, however, will not forget. The rather lonely, flat landscape of creeks and marshes and rivers will stay in the mind, as will the characters whose existence and personality and adventures are influenced by this landscape.*

Some Books by
KATHLEEN PEYTON

THE EDGE OF THE CLOUD. Illus. by Victor G. Ambrus. Cleveland: World, 1969. 207p.
    When Christina and William run away from Uncle's house in *Flambards*, Christina stays with Aunt Grace in London while William

finds a job at a flying field as a mechanic. When a job as receptionist becomes available at a hotel near the field, Christina takes the job and moves there to be nearer William. Eventually William moves up to become a test pilot for the new experimental planes, and Christina learns to share his excitement while attempting to bury her terror of the danger each time he flies. The two of them are married a few days after Britain enters World War I, and the story ends with William about to enter the Royal Flying Corps.

Awarded Carnegie Medal, 1969.

FLAMBARDS. Illus. by Victor G. Ambrus. Cleveland: World, 1967. 206p.
Orphaned Christina, having lived with a succession of aunts, has come to live with Uncle Russell and her cousins Mark and William. Uncle and arrogant Mark are fanatic riders; William despises it. When a hunting accident ends William's riding days, he becomes fascinated with the new science of flying and works secretly on an experimental airplane. Uncle's unwillingness to recognize that the world is changing—both socially and materially—in these days just before World War I, brings him into conflict with William and Christina and a young groomsman who befriends the two of them. His cruelty and intransigence result in a breakup which sends William and Christina away to make new lives for themselves and to plan marriage in the future.

FLAMBARDS IN SUMMER. Illus. by Victor G. Ambrus. Cleveland: World, 1969. 189p.
After Will's death in action and the report that Mark is missing, Christina returns to Flambards. It is somewhere to go, she believes, to pick up the pieces of her life and to occupy herself beyond thinking. Now in possession of her father's money, she hopes to farm the place and make it live again. With the birth of Will's child, her adoption of Mark's illegitimate son, and Dick's return to help, Flambards begins to seem like a home again. Christina has just realized that she loves Dick when Mark turns up, and she is faced with resolving all the complications that his reappearance brings about.

FLY-BY-NIGHT. Illus. by the Author. Cleveland: World, 1968. 189p.
o.p.; Archway, paper.
Pony-mad Ruth is told that she may have a pony when her family moves from London to a housing estate in the country. She discovers that her forty pounds savings will buy only an untrained two-year-

old. Ruth's trials and errors in training Fly (she has never ridden before) and finding money for food and harness make it a tough year. As family finances become more and more stretched, her father decides they must sell the house and move to a flat. Happily, they find an old two-acre farm which is within their means, and Ruth may keep her pony.

The portrayal of Ruth and her family and of Ruth's joys and agonies with Fly make the story very real.

THE MAPLIN BIRD. Illus. by Victor G. Ambrus. Cleveland: World, 1965. 237p. o.p.

Emily and her brother Toby have run away from a cruel aunt and uncle and are living aboard an old fishing smack. When Emily goes to work as a maid to wealthy Mrs. Seymour, she is attracted to Adam, Mrs. Seymour's ne'er-do-well son. But Adam, Emily soon learns, is in the serious business of smuggling. She watches with growing concern as her brother Toby becomes involved in Adam's schemes and as she herself falls more under his spell. A final disaster brings Toby to his senses and Emily to a realization that she will be able to forget Adam.

A PATTERN OF ROSES. Illus. by the Author. New York: Crowell, 1972. 186p.

When Tim and his parents move from London to the country, he discovers several drawings by a boy who had once lived in their house. Tim has a supernatural awareness of the boy, and this—with the help of the Vicar's daughter—makes it possible for him to un- earth the mystery of the boy's life and early death. At the same time, Tim is trying to decide whether to bow to his father's choice of a career or to pursue his own talent in art. As he learns about the boy and tries to understand him, he is able to make a decision about himself.

THE PLAN FOR BIRDSMARSH. Illus. by Victor G. Ambrus. Cleveland: World, 1966. 239p. o.p.

Paul looks forward with deep content to a future on his family's coastal farm, until he learns that a projected marina to be built on the site will kill his plans. But there is a more frightening problem which forces into the background his concern over the marina. His older brother Chris is experimenting with a sea survival suit. Paul suspects that the two men working with Chris are sabotaging the suit, in which case Chris will be drowned in a survival test. It is Paul, however, who by accident is forced to test the suit when his old smack is wrecked. After facing the loneliness and terror of surviving for thirty-three hours in the cold sea, Paul finds he has the self-confidence and maturity to face the reality of losing the farm and going on from there.

SEA FEVER. Illus. by Victor G. Ambrus. Cleveland: World, 1962. 240p. When his father drowns off their fishing boat, Matt inherits responsibility for his family. He also inherits the enmity of Beckett, a local fisherman/smuggler. Matt finds that everything he does feeds Beckett's hostility, until Matt is finally in fear for his life. Overburdened and lonely, Matt is fortunate in gaining the friendship and respect of a wealthy yacht owner and his son. It is their friendship, coupled with Matt's strength and integrity, that turns the tide in Matt's favor and sets him in the right direction.

THUNDER IN THE SKY. Illus. by Victor Ambrus. Cleveland: Collins, 1967. 160p.
The time is the First World War, and fifteen-year-old Sam, mate on a barge carrying military supplies across the Channel, is too young to enlist. He is proud of his brother Manny who is fighting in France and cannot understand why his brother Gil, mate on another barge, does not enlist. There are rumors that some of the barges are used for spying against England. Sam is horrified to learn that Gil has become innocently involved with a ring of spies and is unable to find a way out of his entanglement. When his ammunition-loaded barge endangers other English ships, Gil finds a heroic but tragic escape from his dilemma.

Barbara Leonie Picard

Barbara Leonie Picard has lived in England all her life. She was educated at boarding school and has lived a quiet life by her own choice. From an early age she wrote stories and short pieces for her own pleasure. Then during World War II she found a purpose in writing and had no difficulty in having her books published.

Most of her books have been written for children and young adults, although she never really considered writing for a particular age group.

Because of her special interest in folk culture of all kinds and in mythology, it is natural that her first books were original fairy stories in the old pattern. Later, she wrote folktales from several countries including England, and she published a retelling of Homer's *Odyssey*. Ancient and medieval history and archaeology are also of special interest to her, and her books reflect these interests.

Her personal likes and dislikes give some insight into her personality. She enjoys nature—trees, flowers, animals ("including slugs, snakes, and mosquitoes"). She likes solitude and all beautiful things, natural and man-made. "I love the past, though I am more or less uninterested in the future." Her most serious dislikes are fear and intolerance. "Fear, because it is and always has been the root of all evil. Intolerance saddens me, because I sincerely believe that 'Comprendre c'est tout pardonner'. I am never tempted to be intolerant about those who are intolerant."

Because of her feeling for nature and wild things, it is understandable that she dislikes to see animals perform. She believes that angling is the most despicable of all the bloodsports because it is one of the least dangerous. Some of her more frivolous dislikes are publicity, housework, sports, and daily newspapers.

Miss Picard enjoys a variety of hobbies such as reading, embroidery, going to the theater, collecting complete recordings of grand opera, and collecting Japanese prints. She continues to devote much of her time to writing.

Interview

During World War II, I started to write. I'd always intended to write, but I never thought of writing children's books at all. During the war we had the duty, which occurred about once a week, called fire-watching. We had to sit up all night in some public building which had to be protected better than private homes because of what went on there, like the hospital, the town hall, or the public library. People got together in groups for each building. They each had a certain area they were supposed to look after. They came at dusk and left the next morning at 8 o'clock. During the night they held themselves ready with fire extinguishers to put out any fires that might be started by incendiary bombs. It wasn't just the mass of planes going over to bomb London, but it often was the single raider. Once a week I used to do this. I read at first while "watching," and then I thought it would be rather nice to use my nights fire-watching in a constructive way. So I started to write stories.

I was always interested in reading legends and folktales of different countries. My first book was not the telling of folktales actually, but an original fairy story in the old pattern, called *The Mermaid and the Simpleton.* Then Oxford University Press asked me to retell Homer's *Odyssey* for their illustrated children's classics series.

> *Out of the hundreds of folktales and legends from a particular country, how do you choose the ones you will include in a collection?*

I try to make it as much a variety of plot as possible. It isn't always easy because so many of these legends have very similar plots. The hero does very much the same things, he gets into the same situations. But you can do it if you search around enough and think hard. That's what I've tried to do with my three collections of British stories. I think, on the whole, I did manage to get quite a good variety about it.

Some of these heroes appear in the folklore of different countries. Not only are there the main stories about these characters, but other legendary heroes get associated with them in some way. For example, sometimes stories about heroes who had nothing to do with King Arthur had their settings in King Arthur's court to make them more interesting. Or in a story where a king was needed as an unpleasant character, the name of Arthur was used. Poor Arthur comes off rather badly. It seems all wrong to us.

Miss Picard discusses the difference between writing fiction and retelling legends and folktales.

Well, you have to keep to the rules. In writing fiction, you can make your characters do just what you like, and you can change your mind halfway if you want to. But with retelling, you mustn't conjecture too much. I always like to stick to the traditional versions even if I use one part of the story from one version and another part from another version. I do this frequently and try to make it more interesting, or more exciting, or a better story. But you still have to stick to something that somebody else has laid down for you perhaps hundreds of years ago. I think that's the main difference—that you must stick to the story in dealing with legends and folktales.

Miss Picard went on to write historical fiction and here she comments about it.

There are three kinds of historical novels. There are the ones written entirely about historical characters, where the author uses all known facts and then conjectures the missing passages in history and then fills them in the best way he can. Then there is the sort which deals partly with fictional characters and partly with historical characters, where the historical personalities are actually people in the book who play a part in the story and have contacts and dealings with the fictitious characters. Then there is the third kind, where you have entirely fictitious characters set against the background of the period. Of the three kinds, I like the last best. If I put in a historical character, he doesn't ever speak. I find the third kind is the most satisfactory to read when other people have written it, so it is the one I have chosen for myself. It's just a matter of personal taste.

Most of my historical novels have been written about a period that I know rather well, the first part of the fourteenth century, and knowing enough about the background, I just go ahead and write the story. I tend to write rather rapidly at the beginning. My own idea—what I call the composition part of the story—is to get it all down on paper regardless of the words I've used. However, as I go along, I put in brackets after anything I'm not absolutely certain of, so that it will help when reading through it. Once the original writing is done, I can sit back and put in the right words, polish up the writing, check on the historical points, and put in alterations. I still check on any questionable points even when I'm pretty certain that I know the right answers, because I think it very important to be thorough and accurate. I do find with this checking at the end, that with every book there is still a small, hard core of facts which can't be verified. In that case, I just have to leave them out, even if it means sacrificing an episode which I would have liked to keep in the book.

It seems to me necessary to plan a book carefully before writing it. Otherwise, you find some parts are overwritten and other parts are too short of their background, and altogether the book seems lopsided when you have finished. So I always do try to plan very carefully. Sometimes I've managed better than others. With *One Is One* I think I managed well.

> ONE IS ONE *has its setting in the Middle Ages, and tells of Stephen, a sensitive, insecure boy who is thought to be a coward. He changed for good as he grew into manhood, and the events in his life influenced his development greatly.*

It's the one I like best of all my books. I had everything planned out very carefully with this book. It's one I'd been wanting to write for three or four years before I actually started. I'd been thinking over the plot and working out the characters. So I was very happy to get down to writing it. I found it particularly satisfying to write. I made it fall into three parts—one for the dog and one for each of the two people who influenced Stephen for good, and how he lost each one of them.

When discussing her book LOST JOHN, *in which John's stepfather was very cruel to him and denied him his rightful inheritance, Miss Picard sketched some of the conditions characteristic of the Middle Ages which she so skillfully weaves into the story.*

There is a very simple reason why John did not revenge himself against his stepfather. I don't think that sort of thing necessarily happens in life. People aren't always able to get their rightful dues, and I think, particularly in the Middle Ages, a great deal of injustice went on and people never got their wrongs righted, and never got their inheritances.

In the Middle Ages when *Lost John* took place, traveling was dangerous not only because of bands of robbers, but because of many other circumstances. The noblemen, the big barons, had their little private armies, and went around fighting each other or repressing the lower classes. And there were very harsh game laws. Often people who had done nothing that we would consider wrong today would find themselves on the wrong side of the law, and they would have to fly from their own homes. The country was so underdeveloped in those days that there were great areas of forest lands where it was very easy to hide yourself. Naturally, it's much easier to get together in a group to live than it is for one person to manage alone. So, there were large bands of men in these forest areas like the Forest of Arden and Sherwood Forest. In a way, these bands of robbers were really not much worse than the barons who were considered respectable and could go to court. I think that was the result of the cruelty of the laws. But then the laws were cruel because it was so very easy to escape after breaking them. The two things fit into each other.

Miss Picard expresses her feelings about writing sequels.

Actually, several people have suggested to me that I should write a sequel to *Lost John*, with the adventures of John and Alan and how John did revenge his wrongs. But I often think that sequels are rather a letdown after the first book. So often the author seems to put all his best into the first book, and then when it comes to the sequel some of the old fire is missing and characters have done all of the developing in the first book.

Miss Picard comments on one of her historical novels of another period.

Another of my historical novels is of a much later period—the eighteenth century. It's called *The Young Pretenders*. It started with an idea I had about a moral problem. When one gives one's word to somebody under a mistaken apprehension that he is other than he is, and then finds out the truth afterwards, is one obliged to keep his word, or, under the circumstances, is he at liberty to break it? The plot circles around that. Two young characters meet somebody whom they think is admirable when he really isn't. They promise to help him, and they promise they won't tell anyone else about him. When they finally discover that he is a criminal, they have a really hard time wondering what to do about it— particularly the boy, who is older than the girl. It was a piece of history I was interested in, but I didn't know as much about the background as I did about the medieval period, so, I had to check many more of the historical points. It was also a period in which I could try to make the characters in the book speak as they would have spoken then. (In the medieval stories I could not use the speech of the period because some people spoke French and others spoke an English we could not understand at all.) But in the eight-eenth-century book I could try to make people speak as they would have spoken because it is not so far removed from our modern speech. I did find that I had to be terribly careful because there are so many novels in that period, and my readers may have read other works of the period written by contemporary authors where the dialogue would be absolutely authentic. So I had to be doubly careful.

I still write for myself as well as for my readers, and I could never write about anything in which I didn't have a personal interest. Once the books are finished and appear in cold print, I can view them objectively and critically and read them with as much enjoyment as though they had been written by another author.

Some Books by
BARBARA LEONIE PICARD

LOST JOHN, A YOUNG OUTLAW IN THE FOREST OF ARDEN. New York: Criterion, 1962. 224p. o.p.

Fifteen-year-old John Fitzwilliam leaves home because his cruel stepfather has denied him his rightful inheritance. Bitter and angry, he sets out to fulfill the oath he took four years before to avenge his father's murder. Wandering aimlessly in the Forest of Arden, he is captured by a band of outlaws, and later nicknamed Lost John. Inevitably, his life becomes involved with the leader of the band, the notorious Ralf the Red, whom he comes to look upon as a father. The story ends with a strange twist of fate.

This historical novel provides adventure and the details of life in the Middle Ages in the reign of King Richard of England.

ONE IS ONE. New York: Holt, 1965. 285p.

Miss Picard chose the title for this historical novel from a line of an English folk song: "One is one and all alone and everymore shall be so." Knighthood was a way of life in fourteenth-century England, a time when physical prowess and bravery were synonymous with manhood. Stephen is a sensitive, insecure boy who is thought to be a coward, and so he is sent to a monastery. After a few unhappy years there, he runs away, still determined to achieve knighthood. Beaten and half-starved, he is befriended by a wise and kind young nobleman who trains Stephen in jousting, riding, and archery. Stephen has never been so happy. For the first time in his life he is accepted, just as he is. His joy does not last, however, and drawing on the wisdom Sir Pagan has imparted to him, he sadly but confidently makes his plans for the future.

RANSOM FOR A KNIGHT. Illus. by C. Walter Hodges. New York: Walck, 1956. 312p.

The author has developed an engrossing novel centered around Alys de Renneville and her servant, Hugh, who go to Scotland carrying the ransom for the release of her father and brother, captured after the battle of Bannockburn. The message that her father and brother are alive is brought to the castle by an injured knight who, after giving the message, briefly lapses into unconsciousness and forgets all that he has said about the ransom to be paid and her father's whereabouts. Alys can convince no one that the message is true, so she determines to go herself, and with some difficulty she persuades Hugh to go with her. They leave secretly and travel the full length of England, carrying the ransom with them.

The book is crowded with characters and incidents set against the background of fourteenth-century England.

THE YOUNG PRETENDERS. Illus. by Victor Ambrus. New York: Criterion, 1966. 231p. o.p.

In secret opposition to their family's political sympathies, two teen-age eighteenth-century English children, Francis and Annabel Rimpole, become infatuated with the young Prince of the House of Stuart. A handsome young man, pursued by the King's soldiers, takes refuge in their garden one day. Francis and Bella are convinced that he is a soldier of Prince Edward Charles. They hide him in the unoccupied Dower House, and go to great lengths of deception to feed him and care for him while he recovers from an injured foot. Both are disillusioned when the soldier's real identity is revealed, but feel the need to protect him in spite of that.

THE FAUN AND THE WOODCUTTER'S DAUGHTER. Illus. by Charles Stewart. New York: Criterion, 1964. 255p.

THE GOLDFINCH GARDEN. Illus. by Anne Linton. New York: Criterion, 1965. 122p. o.p.

THE MERMAID AND THE SIMPLETON. Illus. by Philip Gough. New York: Criterion, 1970. 258p.

Miss Picard has written these three collections of original fairy tales in the old pattern so that they carry the magic of the traditional tale.

Retellings of Folktales and Legends

In retelling these ancient traditional tales, Miss Picard has made a fine contribution to the body of folk literature. In most of the collections, the author has given brief notes about each story and its background.

CELTIC TALES; LEGENDS OF TALL WARRIORS AND OLD ENCHANTMENTS. Illus. by John G. Galsworthy. New York: Criterion, 1964. 159p. o.p.
> A collection of some of the good Celtic tales omitted from *Tales of the British People* and *Hero Tales from the British Isles*.

FRENCH LEGENDS, TALES, AND FAIRY STORIES. Illus. by Joan Kiddell-Monroe. New York: Walck, 1955. 216p.
> Tales of the French epic heroes, tales from the French court in the Middle Ages, and legends from the French provinces.

GERMAN HERO-SAGAS AND FOLK-TALES. Illus. by Joan Kiddell-Monroe. New York: Walck, 1958. 197p.
> Sagas of heroes such as Gudrun, Dietrich of Bern, and Siegfried, and tales of lesser men, such as the Ratcatcher of Hamelin, and Till Eulenspiegel.

HERO TALES FROM THE BRITISH ISLES. Illus. by John G. Galsworthy. New York: Criterion, 1963. 159p. o.p.
> Stories of the folk heroes of the British Isles, for example: Robin Hood from England, Taliesen from Wales, Finn McCool from Scotland, and Cuchulain from Ireland.

STORIES OF KING ARTHUR AND HIS KNIGHTS. With wood engravings by Roy Morgan. New York: Walck, 1955. 292p.
> The tales are chosen from Malory and other sources.

TALES OF THE BRITISH PEOPLE. Illus. by Eric Fraser. New York: Criterion, 1961. 159p. o.p.
> As noted in the preface, these are "stories brought to the British Isles by different people who settled there: Iberians, Celts, Romans, Saxons, Danes, and Normans—all of those who eventually blended together to form the British people of today."

TALES OF THE NORSE GODS AND HEROES. Illus. by Joan Kiddell-Monroe. New York: Oxford, 1953. 312p.
> The first part of the book is devoted to tales of the Norse gods; the second part concentrates on tales of the Norse heroes.

Rosemary Sutcliff

Born in 1920 in England, Rosemary Sutcliff moved frequently in her early years. Her father was a naval officer, and she and her mother changed homes as often as he was transferred.

When she was two she became ill, and as a result had to spend a number of years in bed. Because this made formal education difficult, she studied at home with her mother and was read to extensively. Among the books read to her were those of Rudyard Kipling and Kenneth Grahame, and these have had a lasting influence.

She began school when she was nine, left at fourteen, and from then on educated herself. Her schooling was not completely over, however, for she attended the Bideford School of Art and became an accomplished painter of miniatures. Her work has been exhibited at the Royal Academy, and she is a member of the Royal Society of Miniature Painters.

Miss Sutcliff began to write when she was twenty-five, and from 1950, when her first children's book was published, she devoted herself exclusively to writing.

She lives in the village of Walberton on the Sussex Downs in a house secluded behind a high wall. The wall is misleading, however, for there is nothing secluded about Rosemary Sutcliff's life. Though her illness left her with impaired mobility, it did not impair her zest for living. Her study is the hub of the household and it is here that she welcomes visitors, watched over by her two dogs, a dignified golden Labrador and an impetuous long-haired Chihuahua. Despite the flow of life through this room, she manages to work here, too, researching and writing in longhand the historical novels which have made her famous.

Interview

Writing historical fiction is one of those things that happened, I suppose, because I had so much read to me when I was small. I don't always enjoy writing. It's too like hard work. But I have no wish to write modern books. I don't think I could write modern books. To me half the fun of writing a book is the research entailed. I love trying to piece together historical background and to catch the right smell of the period. Every period has very much its own subtle difference in smell, and the whole atmosphere changes a little bit every few years through history. It's a fascinating exercise to try and catch this difference.

Usually I prepare myself by getting a great many books together from the county library. This acts like a snowball. Every book has a bibliography and I get a great many more books from each bibliography. I just go on until I am completely embedded in the period and place that I'm writing about. Generally the plot comes from the historical background, not the other way around. The two things gradually move together in my mind as I get the research further, so that the plot grows with it, if plot it can be called—I'm not very good at plots. They just grow fairly naturally, side by side.

I suppose I've always had a particular interest in the time of the Roman occupation of Britain. I was brought up on Rudyard Kipling's *Puck of Pook's Hill*, notably the three Roman stories. They seemed to me quite marvelous. At that time I didn't really understand what they were about and didn't know what the Roman Empire was, but I loved them and they had a sort of magic for me. I think for this reason when I started to write my own books, they automatically gravitated towards Roman Britain.

Two of the Roman Britain stories are THE EAGLE OF THE NINTH *and* THE MARK OF THE HORSE LORD. *In each of them the hero becomes involved in the superstitions and tribal practices of the primitive people of what is now northern Scotland. As Marcus and Phaedrus discovered, life beyond Hadrian's Wall was very different from that of Roman Britain.*

These people were Celts, and the Celt is very different from the Roman. Romans are very like the modern Anglo-Saxon in some ways. They are very down-to-earth, straightforward people who think in straight lines. The Celt is the chap who has the imagination and who thinks in curves. He takes right off—he takes both feet off the ground at once and takes off into the blue. I think that the basic difference is that the Celts were at a very much earlier state of civilization. They were tribesmen and they worshipped much more primitive gods. They had much more faith in magic and ritual and in the dark sort of secret side of things than the Romans had. So neither of them could understand the other at all.

I keep a little red exercise book with notes and get a new one each time I'm writing a book. In this I write down all that I'm going to write about the characters, real and imaginary. I gradually think these people out, what their personal appearance is going to be, any kind of odd tricks and habits and likes and dislikes that they've got, their backgrounds, anything I can think of that makes them into real people, so that if one walked around behind them they would have a back view as well as a front view. By the time I've got all this locked together, they've become kind of acquaintances. As I write about them, I get to know them better. By the time I've finished a book, our acquaintance has ripened and I know them as one knows a person whom you've known through the years and got to know very well. If I make them do something out of character, I know instantly: "But that isn't how Marcus would react to the particular circumstance. There's a wrong tone here somewhere. It's got to be put right. He wouldn't have said that—it's not in his character." I know it as I would know it about a person that I knew well, but it's something that happens of its own accord.

> *Marcus, Phaedrus, Beric, Drem, Randal, Owain—all the main characters are boys. There are often girls in the stories and they are strongly portrayed, but they act as minor characters.*

It just always happens like that. I think I've got where I can understand boys better than I do girls. I did once try to write one in which a girl was the main character—that was *The Shield Ring.* Then, of course, even in that it switched from the girl to the boy.

The Shield Ring began because friends were spring cleaning. In getting things out of their attic, they dug out a little paperback book that somebody had written twenty or thirty years ago about a sort of Norse pocket, a settlement of Norsemen in the Lake District in Norman times. It told about the tremendous resistance these Norsemen put up to the Norman invasion. This fascinated me. I was halfway through another book at the time. But this idea fascinated me so much that the other book went dead on me and I had to drop it and start this one. It's a kind of subject which is really a readymade book in itself: a small enclosed sea of action like this, an enclosed society, and a kind of rearguard action as well. I always like rearguard actions—they make good story material. The story just grew from that. I was able to get a lot of books about the north country which helped me greatly. Sometimes you find certain parts of the country are not well documented, and it is much more difficult to catch the atmosphere of the countryside. But the Lake District of England was very well documented. There were lots of books that evoked the countryside and the sights and sounds and smells vividly. So I was able to get very deeply into it and I enjoyed writing it.

I think *The Eagle of the Ninth* is my favorite among my books. I think and hope that I have written better books since, but you know you don't love people for their brilliance or anything of this sort. *The Eagle of the Ninth* has always been my favorite and probably always will be. I think I'm so fond of it because when I wrote it I was going into the hospital to have an operation. I'd had quite a lot before but they'd been a long time before and I was out of practice. You can get out of practice with operations. I was scared stiff and I wanted, really, someone to keep me company. I created Marcus and had him for a companion. I've always felt rather special towards him, as though he was a friend who's been with me in a tough corner.

History is a continuous process. You know, in history books, history has been chopped up into little static pictures. But it isn't like that. It's a continuous process, like a tree growing or a river. I think it's important to children today because it's how we got to be where we are now. You can't properly understand where you are now if you don't know how you grew to be there—what your roots are, where you came from. Because we're still part of history. It's not complete unless you see what's behind you.

This sense of history speaks clearly to us in Rosemary Sutcliff's books. In DAWN WIND, *we are in the Dark Ages. Owain has spent bitter years as a thrall. But as the story ends, he is aware of himself as a part of history. He can look back and see the last of the light before the dark set in and ahead the dawn wind stirring: "Deep within him . . . was a sense of change, like the change in the wind at winter's end."*

Some Books by
ROSEMARY SUTCLIFF

BEOWULF. Illus. by Charles Keeping. New York: Dutton, 1961. 93p.
> A retelling of the legend of the Geatish hero Beowulf. The slaying of the monster Grendel, the battle with the hag Sea-Woman and the final tragic struggle with the Fire-Drake are given a strong and epiclike telling.

THE CAPRICORN BRACELET. Illus. by Richard Cuffari. New York: Walck, 1973. 149p.
> The story of a soldiering family of Roman Britain is told in six episodes covering the years from A.D. 61 to A.D. 383. A military bracelet for distinguished conduct in battle is won by the first Lucius to serve in the Eagles. The episodes in the family's history are linked by this bracelet as it is handed down to the soldier of each generation.

DAWN WIND. Illus. by Charles Keeping. New York: Walck, 1961. 241p.
> It is the sixth century A.D. The Dark Ages have begun. The Roman legions are gone and Britain is being laid waste by the Saxon invaders. With his family dead at the hands of the Saxons, Owain starts north. When he comes upon another refugee, they travel together.

In exchange for her safekeeping, Owain sells himself into thrall-dom. The years that follow are bitter, but at the end of them he can see the light ahead.

THE EAGLE OF THE NINTH. Illus. by C. Walter Hodges. New York: Walck, 1954. 255p.

In A.D. 117 the Ninth Legion, with Marcus's father as commander, had marched off to Caledonia and never returned. Ten years later, Marcus and his freed slave set out on the long journey beyond Hadrian's Wall to solve the mystery of the lost legion and to bring back their eagle standard. The truth he finds is bitter but Marcus learns to accept it and to value loyalty and friendship.

HEATHER, OAK, AND OLIVE. Illus. by Victor Ambrus. New York: Dutton, 1972. 120p.

Three stories celebrating friendship. In the first, the chief's daughter Nessan saves an Irish captive from a sacrificial death. Roman Britain is the setting for the second story in which a medic in the Cavalry saves the honor of a young pennant-bearer. The third story tells of two competitors, an Athenian and a Spartan, who become friends at the Olympic Games. In their race with each other and in its aftermath, they understand the gift of friendship.

KNIGHT'S FEE. Illus. by Charles Keeping. New York: Walck, 1962. 241p.

Randal, hound boy for Hugh Goch at Arundel Castle, is taken as varlet by Sir Everard to be brought up with his grandson Bevis. The friendship between the two boys grows strong and when Bevis is knighted, Randal becomes his squire. Randal's loyalty to Sir Everard's family and to others he loves wins knighthood for him.

THE LANTERN BEARERS. Illus. by Charles Keeping. New York: Walck, 1959. 252p.

When the Roman legions withdraw from Britain, it is a time of decision for many of the British-born legionnaires. Torn between fidelity to Rome and love for their birthplace, they must make a choice between the two. Aquila is one who chooses to stay and fight to save a divided Britain from the Saxon invaders.

Awarded the Carnegie Medal, 1959.

THE MARK OF THE HORSE LORD. New York: Walck, 1965. 305p.

In Roman Britain in the second century, Phaedrus the Gladiator wins his wooden foil in the arena and is given his freedom. But his resemblance to Midir, Lord of the Horse People, is noticed and he is persuaded to impersonate Midir and seek revenge against the enemy who has taken Midir's throne. Phaedrus's new life among the tribesmen of northern Britain leads to danger and adventure and, ultimately, to fulfillment.

OUTCAST. Illus. by Richard Kennedy. New York: Walck, 1955. 229p.
Beric, infant son of Roman parents, is washed ashore from a shipwreck on the British coast. Despite the prediction that he will bring a curse upon them, he is adopted by a man and a woman of a British tribe. Cast out by the tribe when bad times come, Beric attempts to join the Roman forces but is enslaved and shipped to Rome. Returning eventually to Britain, seemingly rejected by the world of men, he finds his own place to belong.

THE SHIELD KING. Illus. by C. Walter Hodges. New York: Walck, 1956. 215p.
High in the Cumberland fells of England's Lake Country, the last of the Norsemen hold out against the Norman conquerors. When there is a need for a spy in the camp of the Normans, Bjorn volunteers for the venture, braving his fear that under torture he might inform against his people.

THE SILVER BRANCH. Illus by Charles Keeping. New York: Walck, 1958. 215p.
After the Roman Command in Britain begins falling into disarray but before the last of the legions are withdrawn, Justin and Flavius are assigned to the Eighth Legion. Discovering a plot to overthrow Carausius, Emperor of Britain, they fail to convince him of its truth and are transferred to an outpost on the Roman wall. The opportunity comes to show their loyalty to Rome and they go to its defense leading a force which marches under the eagle standard of the lost Ninth Legion.

WARRIOR SCARLET. New York: Walck, 1958. 240p.
Drem, because of his lame arm, cannot fulfill the wolf killing requirement which will make him a warrior in his Bronze Age tribe. His place must be with the Half People, a more primitive tribe that herds the sheep for Drem's own people. When at length he is accepted back by his tribesmen, Drem finds that his exile has changed him profoundly.

THE WITCH'S BRAT. Illus by Richard Lebenson. New York: Walck, 1970. 143p.

His dead grandmother's reputation as a witch, together with his own twisted leg and hunched shoulder, are reason enough for superstitious neighbors to stone Lovel from the village. Found starving and ill by a swineherd, Lovel is taken to the monastery near Winchester where he is cared for by the brothers and where he remains to do the odd jobs no one else wanted. Rahere, the King's Jongleur, is the first to glimpse Lovel's worth, but it is Brother Anselm who discovers Lovel's healing gift and gives him the opportunity to work at his skill. When Rahere, now turned monk, is determined to found a hospital for the poor, Lovel joins him and finds his place as "one of the menders of this world."

Three of Miss Sutcliff's books of Roman Britain form a sequence: *The Eagle of the Ninth*, *The Silver Branch*, and *The Lantern Bearers*.

Brian Wildsmith. Photograph courtesy of Oxford University Press.

Brian Wildsmith

Brian Wildsmith and his two brothers were raised in a small mining town in northern England. At the age of ten, Brian received a scholarship to attend a school in nearby Sheffield where chemistry seemed to be his primary interest. For a time, he thought he wanted to make that his career. But a few years later he discovered that he had artistic ability and what he really wanted to do was to express himself through painting. This opened a new world to him, and he soon transferred to Barnsley School of Art. It was here that he received a scholarship to the Slade School of Fine Art at the University of London, where he studied for three years. After spending two years in military service and three years teaching in a grammar school (equivalent to a United States high school), he decided to try free-lancing.

It was Mabel George, former Children's Book Editor of Oxford University Press, who really recognized his ability and creativity. Recalling her reaction to a few paintings he brought with him on his first visit to her office, she says, "Looking at the abstract paintings, I saw how boldly, yet delicately, the color was used, how poetically and simply the imagination behind the painting was expressed."[1] It was Miss George who gave Mr. Wildsmith his start in illustrating books for children. She has continued to encourage him in his work and publish his picture books. Of the hopes she had for him she writes: "Without divulging the hopes we had set upon him, we let him learn the discipline of the book through pen and ink illustrations, and the occasional jacket. When the time was right, we asked him to make some color plates for a new edition

1. Mabel George, "Brian Wildsmith," *The Calendar* of the Children's Book Council, Fall-Winter (1974–75).

of 'The Arabian Nights.' The reviewers reacted strongly: some with praise, one with violent hostility. That decided it! We knew then that he was 'the one.' We invited him to make his first picture book, an ABC."[2]

In 1962 he received the Kate Greenaway Medal for the outstanding picture book of the year, *Brian Wildsmith's ABC*. In 1963 his *Lion and the Rat* and *Oxford Poetry Book for Children* were runners-up for the Kate Greenaway Medal, as was his *Birds* in 1967. *Birds* was also named by the *New York Times* among the best illustrated children's books for 1967. In 1968 he was runner-up for the Hans Christian Andersen Award for illustrators. His picture books have been published in at least seven countries, including the United States, Switzerland, Sweden, Holland, Germany, and South Africa. He illustrated Christmas cards for UNESCO in 1965. Several million copies were sold around the world.

This remarkable talent had its subtle beginnings in the little mining town of Penistone. Mr. Wildsmith's father worked in the coal mines, but painting was his hobby. The evenings he could spend with his paints and brushes were sheer enjoyment for him after a long day in the pits. Carrying on the tradition, Mr. Wildsmith's daughter, Rebecca, has won a prize for painting in France.

One of Mr. Wildsmith's most recent assignments is quite different from anything else he has done. He was commissioned to design the sets and costumes for a spectacular musical film, *The Blue Bird*, that had its premiere Christmas, 1975. That he should be in some way involved with a musical is quite natural, because he loves music and is an accomplished pianist.

A world traveler, Mr. Wildsmith makes friends wherever he goes. His warmth and understanding, his love and respect for people as individuals, reaches out to them. When he appeared on a BBC television program, the pictures and letters the children sent him afterward were delivered to him in truckloads. When he left Tokyo, several hundred people went to the airport at dawn to bid him goodbye. But with all the acclaim he has received, his friends say he remains the pleasant, friendly, and thoughtful man he has always been.

2. *Ibid.*

Interview

Books have always fascinated me, but the book publishing field seemed like a very closed shop, and I wondered how I might get a start making pictures for books. Then I read somewhere that in England 29,000 titles, on an average, are published every year. Well, it seemed that the thing to do was to design book wrappers. I reasoned out that the cost of making books must be quite expensive. The prices of illustrations and printing them would be so expensive that the publisher would be unwilling to stake this amount of money on someone without experience, such as I. I reasoned that book wrappers would be the thing because it's one picture rather than thirty or forty pictures for a book. This worked and in the end, after three years, I gave up teaching because I could make a living out of book wrappers—not a very good living, but enough. I did a reasonable amount of work for Oxford University Press. I had shown them my paintings earlier. In later years they did tell me that what they were waiting for was the right time to launch out in color books.

In 1960 they asked me to make fourteen color plates for *The Arabian Nights*. The pictures received severe negative criticism from the Times Literary Supplement in London, and I felt sure that Oxford University Press, publishers of the book, would no longer be interested in my work. "Well," I thought, "that's the end of you, Wildsmith." But I hadn't reckoned on Oxford. I think most publishers would have said "Go away," but Oxford really are publishers. They make a decision and they stick to it, and they back their decisions. I will be eternally grateful to them for it. They showed courage as well, and we've had a wonderful relationship. In a sense we trust each other. They trust my judgment and I trust theirs. So we're very happy partners.

After that they asked me for my ideas on ABC's. That really was the start. The *ABC* seemed to break the barrier, and from then on we've never looked back.

Mr. Wildsmith explains how and why the La Fontaine fables were chosen for him to illustrate.

The trouble about printing these lovely full-color picture books is the enormous cost involved. You need a fantastic amount of capital. There is a kind of saturation point, particularly in England, for the sale of some of these color books. Ideally you need international publishing among American and a few European countries.

Then you get the question of idea. What is right for one country may not be right for another country. So you need an international idea. We hit upon this idea of the La Fontaine fables which had never been illustrated in the form of a picture book before. They are timeless stories, with a beginning, middle, and end within a very few lines. They are wonderful ideas, compactly expressed. They fitted our need beautifully.

Then it was up to me. I spent a long time looking through La Fontaine, and I thought, "My goodness, there is nothing here," because some are a bit ribald, you know, and they are mostly political. I think in the end, from several hundred, I sorted out five or six that could be made into picture books for children.

In *The Miller, the Boy and the Donkey*, I made the donkey the main character. We go to Spain as often as we can. It is the country of donkeys, or it used to be. In fact, I took a trip across the Pyrenees looking for a donkey. A friend of mine knew a farmer who had a marvelous donkey. We got the donkey, and I got all the information from him. Contrary to most people's opinion about donkeys, they are not stupid. They are highly intelligent. We taught the donkey to do all kinds of tricks. He stood on his hind legs, and he took the children for rides on his back. He was really wonderful. I have a lovely movie film about him.

Although the Wildsmiths love Spain and spend as much time as possible there, the brilliant colors in which Mr. Wildsmith so often works are, he believes, more English than Spanish.

Most people think of England as a rather misty, mysterious sort of place, the colors not very bright; but really it's a very colorful place. We get the fog and the rain, but when that clears and the sun comes through, the color of the countryside is absolutely intense. Whereas, if you go abroad into the hot countries where the colors are supposed to be absolutely vibrant, it's so hot that you can't see the colors. There is sort of a heat mist and everything becomes faint; the colors fade out. But in England, the half-light brings out the intense color. I think they are very English—my books.

Mr. Wildsmith discusses his reason for working in brilliant colors so frequently, and gives an opinion about quality in picture books.

Brilliant colors do appeal to me, and I think they definitely appeal to children. I don't think they are necessarily more beautiful than the subdued colors. I think a professional artist should be able to work in whatever scale he feels is right for what he is doing. It is like a composer. He has to be able to pick the right key for what it is he is expressing. He's got to be able to work in the whole range and scale. Although I do think that the brilliant range in the color scale does have an attraction for children, I can work equally as well in the lower scale, but somehow, my subject seems to demand the brighter scale. A lot of picture book artists are throwing a lot of bright color together, expecting this to look beautiful. This does not necessarily happen. For example, you can have a red and a green, and they can be absolutely revolting because they act against each other, the two colors. Yet you can do it again in such a way that the amount of red and the amount of green somehow become absolutely glorious together, and they sing, one against the other. This is one of the dangers of color work.

There are some very fine artists working in picture books today, but very few very lovely picture books are being made. There is a demand for beautiful picture books, because many believe that only the very finest should be offered to young children. It's no good waiting until they are twelve before they are given a little culture. They should be brought up with it, so they can distinguish between the quality books and the mediocre, pseudo-quality books. Unfortunately, we are getting too many mediocre pseudo-quality books; they clog the market. They're coming out in thousands. The people in authority can't wade through all those books. They must rely on the reviewers. The reviews in England are in most cases very, very poor because the people who review, in my opinion, just don't know. Consequently, I think perhaps some of the worthwhile books get left behind.

Mr. Wildsmith comments further about illustrating children's books.

There are two kinds of illustration. There is the factual, diagrammatic type of illustration which is fine in its own right. It does its own particular job. Then there is the creative illustration. In the past few years certain artists have begun to really create for children, and their creative illustrations have caused a minor revolution in books for children.

Some kinds of books are more difficult to illustrate than others. Mother Goose presented a few problems—one in particular, for example:

> Oh, where, oh, where has my little dog gone?
> Oh, where, oh, where, can he be?
> With his ears cut short and his tail cut long,
> Oh, where, oh, where can he be?

I had to solve that problem. I had to solve the rhyme before I could make a picture of it. If you look in [my] Mother Goose, you'll see how it's been solved. There is that sort of problem with poetry sometimes, too.

I've always had the opinion that illustrating books should be rather like playing the piano. You don't interpret Bach in the same way you play Chopin. To each you give a different interpretation, and each book should have its own appearance which is different from any other book. The difficulty is to make the two things, the book and the picture, absolutely one. To make them so right that there is no other way it can be done.

As an artist, Mr. Wildsmith creates his pictures for books with great care, and not only extends the text, but gives each picture a beauty and vibrance of its own. Perhaps his 1, 2, 3 is the best example of this kind of book. It is significant to note here that Mr. Wildsmith has been deeply influenced by Rembrandt, Goya, Paul Klee, and Piero della Francesca. He commented on his approach.

The creative illustration for children may be a thing in its own right, standing independent of words. A book doesn't have to be a book of words. It is a book, and the language is color and form, not a written symbol.

What are his aims when writing and illustrating books for children?

Even if children don't react immediately to my books, somehow, I hope that I may sow a cultural germ in their artistic digestive systems which will one day flower and bear fruit.

A Talk for Children

Mr. Wildsmith very graciously agreed to record some comments about his work that could be used directly with children.

Hello, boys and girls. As I am speaking to you, I am a long, long, way away from you. I think it must be about 3,000 miles. It's difficult to imagine, isn't it? I'm sitting in a little house in a garden in the middle of London, surrounded by trees, and there are little squirrels and little birds in that garden. We have a little robin that lives in the garden. He's always pecking at my flowers. I have a very beautiful flower called an azalea, and he's always picking the flower buds off the azalea. Today is a very beautiful day. The sun is shining and the birds are twittering away, and I am now going to tell you a little bit about my picture books.

I have illustrated quite a few picture books. The first book I illustrated was called *The ABC*, and then I illustrated four books called, *The Lion and the Rat*, *The North Wind and the Sun*, *The Hare and the Tortoise*, and *The Rich Man and the Shoemaker*. I've done a book of nursery rhymes which was called *Mother Goose*, a book of poems called *A Child's Garden of Verses*, a book of *Bible Stories*, and also a book of *Birds*, one of *Wild Animals*, and one called *Fishes*. Now, I don't know if you are like me, but I love drawing and painting, and I enjoyed making all these pictures, and I made them all for young boys and girls like you.

I have four children. I have three girls and a little boy. The oldest girl is called Clare, then Rebecca, and then Anna, who is very cheeky. Then my son is Simon, and he is cheekier still. He can be a very naughty boy. They all like looking at books, and they all help me with my picture books. What happens is, I'm working in my little house in the garden, called a studio, and they come running home from school, open the door, and they say, "Let's have a look at it, Daddy." So, they come in and they look at the painting I've done. I say, "Well, do you like it?" They might say, "Well, it's all right." Then I know it isn't because they are not really excited about it. Then I think, "Oh, you children, you just don't know." So, I just pin it up on my board, and I look at it for about three days, and I think, "Well, perhaps they're right, you know. It's not really very good." So then I start again. They come again, and this time if they get excited and say "Oh, I do like that," then I know it's all right. Then I can go on to the next picture. This is how I can judge, you see, if they are right for young children. What's going to happen when all my children grow up? I don't know. I'll have to have some more, shan't I? And perhaps they will have little children, too, when they grow older.

I suppose I use the same sort of paints as you use to make pictures. I use those in a tube. I have one in my hand now. It's called gouache. I'll spell it for you. It's g-o-u-a-c-h-e, and it comes in tubes. You know that you can do anything with it. You can mix it thick, or you can have it thin. It also dries very quickly. I once started using oil paints, but, of course, oil paint takes a long, long time to dry, so that's no good at all because I have to send my paintings to a printer. If the paint is still not dry, then it just gets smudged. An oil painting can take three or four months to dry, you know, while the gouache will dry in a few minutes, so it's absolutely perfect. I just use ordinary brushes, and I use my finger to paint with sometimes, or a piece of cloth, or, in fact, anything that will make a mark. You don't have to use a brush, you know, to paint. Have you heard of a painter called Rembrandt? I'm sure you have because he was one of the world's finest painters, and in fact, he hardly ever used a brush. Most of the time he used his finger, which is really all you need. I mean, a brush is only something with which to put the paint on the paper or canvas, and your finger will do just the same. The only thing you have to be careful of is that you don't wipe your hands down your clothes. Otherwise, your mother may get very cross.

Most picture books are about 11¼ inches long by 8¾ inches wide, and a painting has to be exactly that size. So if I make the painting larger or smaller, it's no good. It has to be made again. Then when you have made it, you might not like it. So, I have to start again. Sometimes I have to do it five or six times. When I make a book it's always fun, because every book I do is different. And, you know, it's lovely to splash around with bright reds, and yellows, and blues, and greens. So every day I love doing my work, and I think this is what's very important. No matter what you do—I suppose really you haven't thought yet what you're going to do when you finish school, how you're going to earn your living—but I've always thought that the best thing to do is to do something that you love doing. I think if you love doing it, you'll do it well. Do it to the best of your ability, and perhaps someday you'll become the best in the world at doing what it is you like best to do.

The illustration for the letter *L* that appears in color in *Brian Wildsmith's ABC* (Oxford University Press, 1962; Franklin Watts, 1963).

Some Books by

BRIAN WILDSMITH

BRIAN WILDSMITH's ABC. New York: Watts, 1962. unp.
Brian Wildsmith's first book is a most unusual ABC to fascinate the small child, with brilliant color and subjects both familiar and unfamiliar.
Awarded the Kate Greenaway Medal, 1962.

BRIAN WILDSMITH's CIRCUS. New York: Watts, 1970. unp.
A magnificently colorful and memorable experience for any child. This is the artist's circus as he remembers it from childhood. Pictures without words.

BRIAN WILDSMITH's 1,2,3's. New York: Watts, 1965. unp.
This is not only a counting book (numbers 1 to 10), but also a simple study in three basic abstract forms: the circle, rectangle, and triangle. Combining these forms and using stunning colors and clever design, he has devised a book that will stimulate and excite the young child and also lead him to think.

BRIAN WILDSMITH's PUZZLES. New York: Watts, 1970. unp.
To his beautiful color and design, Mr. Wildsmith adds a brain teaser on each page. The puzzles range from the simplest question of choice ("Which color do you like the best?") to the need for a specific answer ("Can you find the nest with only one egg in it?").

BRIAN WILDSMITH's BIRDS. New York: Watts, 1967. unp.

BRIAN WILDSMITH's FISHES. New York: Watts, 1968. unp.

BRIAN WILDSMITH's WILD ANIMALS. New York: Watts, 1967. unp.
Fascinated by the endless variety of terms the English language offers for groups of animals, birds, and fishes, Mr. Wildsmith chose the term he thought best suited each creature included in these books. All are handsomely illustrated.

THE LAZY BEAR. New York: Watts, 1974. unp.
A selfish, pleasure-loving bear bullies his friends into pulling a wagon up the hill for him, so that he can have the fun of riding down. He never offers them a ride and soon they revolt. They push

him over the top and down the other side. Bear apologizes to his friends and all is well again.

The amusing animals in the brilliant illustrations may well distract the reader's attention from the moral of the story.

THE LITTLE WOOD DUCK. New York: Watts, 1972. unp.
The youngest wood duck swims round and round in circles. No matter what his mother teaches him, he cannot swim in a straight line. His brothers and sisters and all the animals around laugh at him and tease him until he is very unhappy. But his swimming in circles saves them all one day when Mr. Fox comes looking for his dinner.

THE OWL AND THE WOODPECKER. New York: Watts, 1972. unp.
The peace of the forest is threatened when owl, who sleeps all day, complains that woodpecker's tapping keeps him awake. The animals devise a plan to force owl to change trees, but that proves unsuccessful. The day comes, however, when owl is very grateful to woodpecker for his tapping, and peace once again returns to the forest.

SQUIRRELS. New York: Watts, 1975. unp.
The model for this book may well be the squirrel in Mr. Wildsmith's garden. The book provides information about the squirrel's home, his eating, how he uses his tail, and how he gathers nuts.

Although the book does not have the interest or variety that some of Mr. Wildsmith's other animal books have, the illustrations have the usual high quality and strong appeal.

THE HARE AND THE TORTOISE. New York: Watts, 1966. unp. o.p.

THE LION AND THE RAT. New York: Watts, 1963. unp. o.p.

THE MILLER, THE BOY, AND THE DONKEY. New York: Watts, 1969. unp. o.p.

THE NORTH WIND AND THE SUN. New York: Watts, 1964. unp. o.p.

THE RICH MAN AND THE SHOEMAKER. New York: Watts, 1966. unp. o.p.
Mr. Wildsmith chooses to retell these La Fontaine fables briefly, in simple language for young children, and brings to each story the magic and color of his art.

Barbara Willard

Barbara Willard had two careers she wanted to pursue—acting and writing. It was difficult to make the choice. Her father was an actor, and when she was a very small child she and her mother went on tour with him. The summer she was eleven, she played the part of a boy in Shakespeare's *Macbeth* when her father was acting at Stratford-on-Avon.

But she had also been writing from a very early age, and although she went into the theater when she finished her formal schooling, eventually she decided to give full time to writing. She wrote prolifically, producing a steady flow of adult novels that received good reviews but had "negligible sales." To supplement her income she wrote scripts for films in the story departments of both American and British companies in London. But always in the back of her mind was a desire to write children's books. She had just never been able to find the right formula.

An adult novel finally led her into the writing of children's books. Miss Willard explains: "Then I wrote a novel called *A Winter in Disguise*. It was about children. Somehow I realized that the best sort of children's book would be just that—a novel about children—but doing things that any child could do, not finding buried treasure or spy-catching or any of those rather worn-out things. *The House with Roots* was the first book I wrote of this kind. It went quite well, so I wrote some more."

Miss Willard and a friend, who also writes, share a charming cottage in the country at the end of a narrow dirt lane. The large picture window in the living room looks out over a beautiful, carefully-tended garden to the broad expanse of Ashdown Forest beyond. A large, black French poodle is her constant companion, and there are cats and goldfish besides.

Her books belie the fact that she was an only child until the age of twelve. Because she had always wished for the companionship of brothers and sisters, she seems to have fulfilled that wish vicariously by writing about large, closely-knit families, a subject which has universal appeal for children. She writes with warmth and understanding, skillfully creating individual personalities and family situations that are realistic and meaningful. Nowhere in the wide range of characters she has created is there a trace of the stereotype.

Interview

I never have a purpose in writing a story except to enjoy myself while I am writing it, and to hope that my readers will enjoy it at the end. Any story that I start has a family or a collection of characters who are there in a way to work out their problems. I don't think I choose the combination of characters. I think that this is something that happens as the story goes along. If I'm writing about a family or about a number of children who live in the same place, then I think that each one of them has to be as important as the other. Probably in those stories I don't have a hero or a heroine, but the whole group is important; and from the group the story develops as they work out their various problems and amusements together. One can only hope that by the end these problems will seem clear to the reader, and that the reader will feel that some purpose has been served. I just write the story as it seems to come to me and as I feel that it is the right way to develop it. Whether I always succeed is another matter. My readers can tell me that.

I enjoy writing about families and family relationships because it was a thing I wanted very much when I was young. Mine was a small family. I was an only child until I was twelve years old, and then I had a brother. He wasn't very much good to me because he was so much younger. Probably we all write about the things we have missed in life.

The way an idea for a book turns up in your mind is usually quite different from the way you finally write the story. You can wake up in the morning with an empty mind, and by the time you go to bed that night, you have a whole book worked out, or you can sit down and write Chapter One, and really and truly you do not know what's going to happen after the end of Chapter One at all. You can't lay down any rules about this. For example, the end of *Grove of Green Holly (Flight to the Forest,* in the United States edition) came about purely by chance really, because I was very stuck on this story. The hero, Rafe, had a problem to resolve. He had to decide how he would continue his life from a certain point of crisis in it. I had no idea myself what his decision would be until his grandmother came from the part of the country where he, Rafe, longed to remain for the rest of his life. This resolved his problem. The story actually worked itself out for me. The allusion to this character (the grandmother) quite by chance, quite unexpectedly, gave me what I hope is a satisfactory ending to the story and to the problem of the hero.

There were a whole lot of things that combined to create the story *Flight to the Forest*. One indeed is the actual physical Grove of Green Holly itself, which is just a few miles away from where I live. It is a vast self-seeded plantation of holly which has become so overgrown and blown by the wind over the years that, when you're inside it, you're inside a room, really. You can hardly see out at all. I often pass that way when I'm walking with my dog in the forest. I often thought how splendid it would be to write something about it, but I didn't know what. There were two other things I wanted to write about. I wanted to write about the forest itself where I live, and how at one time it was the center of the English iron industry before there was coal, when iron was made by smelting with charcoal in furnaces. It was in this area that all this mining and smelting took place. Later on, of course, the iron industry moved to the north of England and they used coal. I was very anxious to write something about this because people know very little about it. It's been forgotten now. Because

I was brought up in the theater—that is to say, my father was an actor, and I was on the stage for a time, and my brother and my cousins, all these people were connected with the theater—I very much wanted to write a story that had something to do with acting. I wanted also to know what had become of the players in that time in English history when Oliver Cromwell was ruling, and when everybody was very stern and puritanical, and they shut down all the theaters because they were considered to be not at all proper. So, I put all these ideas together, and they turned into the story *The Grove of Green Holly*.

I gathered background information for it in the way one always gathers background information—out of books written by other people. Everything that's ever happened in the world, really, can be found in some book or other. When I start researching a subject or a period, one book leads to another. The author of one book almost always alludes to others. So you gradually trace your way from title to title, making copious notes on the way, until you have a clear picture of that period. At least, this is what I do.

In *Storm from the West* I chose to have two families, one from Great Britain and one from the United States, because I had thought for a very long time that it would be a good idea to write about two families who were forced to mingle in this way. I was unable to do this until, in fact, I had been to America, because I didn't feel that I could write about an American family until I had actually seen and particularly listened to one and had seen them together in their relationship, one with another. I went to America, where I spent a month, which I enjoyed so much. Then I came home and wrote *Storm from the West*.

Now, *The Richleighs of Tantamount* was one of those stories that happened absolutely bang. It wasn't only that when I woke up in the morning I didn't know anything about it, but I didn't even know anything about it until lunchtime! I went to London, and it just happened that I was in conversation with somebody who put some tiny little word (and I can't tell you now what it was) into my mind, and I thought I would like to write a story about a family who had everything, and whether it was worthwhile having everything. By the time I came home, as I was driving home in my motorcar about four hours later, I knew everything that happened in that book and also what it was called. That never happened to me before.

I wrote *The Family Tower* and *The Toppling Towers* because I wanted an enormous family story. I wanted a long book about a very big family, and how, living always in one place because their family work was there, they relied on one another. There were lots of cousins and aunts and uncles. Unfortunately my publisher over here thought that the book as I wanted to write it would be too long, and would be too expensive to produce, and that none of you would buy it. So I wrote it in two parts. *The Family Tower* is the first one. *The Toppling Towers* is the second book, but it isn't strictly speaking a sequel. It's a continuation of the first book. So long as you read the first book you know exactly where you are. People coming into the second book without having read the first may wonder who all the characters are. The thing to do is to read *The Family Tower* first.

It seems as though I've always been interested in writing. I suppose I was about seven when I started being interested in writing and reading. But no matter how much you write, there are terrible moments when you feel you'll never write again because you can't think of anything. Although I wrote a number of grown-up novels, I always wanted to write for children. I made many attempts but I always failed. Then quite suddenly (I don't know what it was), I somehow just hit something, and it all started. This was very exciting. Of course, at the beginning so many ideas come you hardly know which one to choose. It's a very thrilling moment. So far, since I've been writing for young readers, I think I've always been at least one step behind an idea. I can say this, that I've been writing for many years, but of all my writing years, the ones I've most enjoyed are the ones spent writing for young people.

Some Books by
BARBARA WILLARD

CHARITY AT HOME. Illus. by Douglas Hall. New York: Harcourt, 1965.
187p. o.p.

To be fourteen and not be sure who your parents are is reason
enough to be temperamental at times. Aunt Joycie, Uncle Steve,
and Charity's cousins make every effort to help her feel that she is
part of their family, but in spite of that, Charity often feels very
much alone. Mr. Tressider, a wealthy neighbor, shows interest in
Charity and in her recently discovered artistic talent. But this, and
Charity's inadvertent disclosure that implicates Derek, a neighbor's
grandson, with a group of thieves, makes her more temperamental
than ever.

This is a realistic story that presents with understanding a girl's
problems in growing up.

A DOG AND A HALF. Illus. by Jane Paton. New York: Nelson, 1971.
128p.

Jill cannot remember when she hasn't wanted a dog. When a sign
appears in the pet shop offering a dog free in return for giving it a
good home, she cannot believe it. She and her friend Limpet go
directly to the dog's owner, Mrs. Remnant, to ask if the offer can
be true. Without discussing it with their parents, the children
return home with Brandy, a lovable and beautiful St. Bernard. It
was a great shock to Jill's parents, but they soon become so attached
to the dog, they decide to keep him. Brandy proves himself an
excellent judge of people when he tracks down a thief whom no
one had suspected.

This is a slight but entertaining story for younger children.

EIGHT FOR A SECRET. Illus. by Lewis Hart. New York: Harcourt, 1960.
219p. o.p.

How can Ellie know when she moves from London to New Barley
that a canoe will play such an exciting part in her life? Ellie is
happy living in London with her brother and sister-in-law since her
parents died, and one of her greatest joys is taking care of her baby
nephew. Ellie doesn't like leaving her friends in London. And what
will she find to do in the country? Old Barleybrook residents re-
sent the new factory and the village of New Barley built for the

workers, but Ellie's new friends come from both towns. A minor accident and a do-it-yourself canoe kit melds the seven boys and girls together into a loyal group with a private project. Secretly launching their new canoe on the Forgotten Lake is the beginning of a busy and exciting summer, climaxed by a never-to-be-forgotten incident that proves their ingenuity, strength, and loyalty to each other.

THE FAMILY TOWER. New York: Harcourt, 1968. 172p. o.p.

THE TOPPLING TOWERS. New York: Harcourt, 1969. 192p. o.p.

These two books are actually one book in two parts and should be read with that in mind. The Towers are a large, closely-knit, well-established family. The motor company that carries the family name has supported four generations of Towers. When Emily, a frail ten-year-old cousin recently orphaned, comes from Africa to live with Jo and Oliver Tower, strange undercurrents and odd rivalries begin to appear within the family. Mystery surrounds Emily, and the tensions mount as the time for the next Towering (meeting of the entire family) approaches. It is Emily's premonition that saves the family from tragedy. Intrigue within the motor company and a threatened take-over of the firm bring the clan together. They work out problems, make decisions, and share the loss of status as gracefully as they can.

Miss Willard has created a remarkable family with a large variety of engaging characters around whom she has woven a realistic and suspense-filled story.

FLIGHT TO THE FOREST. Illus. by Gareth Floyd. New York: Doubleday, 1967. 192p. o.p.

A grove of green holly trees in Ashdown Forest becomes a theater and a refuge for Shakespearean actor Gregory Trundle, his daughter, and her two children, Rafe and Gilia, when Cromwell takes over the rule of England. The Puritans close playhouses all over England and throw many actors in jail. Gregory, growing old now, but still passionately devoted to the theater, instills in Rafe the belief that the theater must be his life, too—in spite of the dangers it now holds. But Rafe, working in an iron forge nearby to support the family, gradually becomes aware that, although he still finds pleasure in acting with his grandfather, his desire to live in this area and make the forge his life's work grows stronger with each day. The conflict builds until, through very realistic circumstances, Rafe is forced to make his final decision.

HETTY. Illus. by Michael Hampshire. New York: Harcourt, 1962. 192p.

Hetty Jebb is thirteen years old the year of Queen Victoria's Jubilee. The middle child of a family of three girls and two boys, Hetty finds it very difficult to be as proper as adults expect her to be. She is quite sure that her red hair is responsible for her hot temper, and for the disposition which gives her the urge to ride the banister from the nursery to the first floor, to play truant from school, and to get into many other predicaments. Yet, when she goes every Tuesday to have tea with her best friend Blanche Verily, a lonely little rich girl, Hetty is very sure they should not indulge in the escapades Blanche invents for them. When Blanche goes off to private school, and a sudden misfortune threatens to bring financial reverses to the Jebb family, Hetty's life takes on new meaning.

Miss Willard got the idea for this charming story from her mother. Hetty is very much like her mother, and many things that happen in the story are based on events in her mother's childhood.

THE POCKET MOUSE. Illus. by Mary Russon. New York: Knopf, 1969. 32p.

An appealing story for younger children about a boy who carries crumbs in his pocket for a stuffed mouse. After Colin finds a live field mouse in his pocket, he senses that a cage or a pocket are too confining for a wild animal. Surprisingly, his rather severe nursemaid seems to understand his feeling, and helps him, in the middle of the night, to return the mouse to its natural habitat. The illustrations are attractive and add much to the story's appeal.

THE RICHLEIGHS OF TANTAMOUNT. Illus. by C. Walter Hodges. New York: Harcourt, 1966. 189p.

Often the Richleigh children looked longingly at the large picture of Tantamount Castle which hung in the drawing room of their Victorian home in London. Often they begged their father to take them to the ancient castle built on the Cornish coast by their great-great-great-grandfather. Now their wish comes true. Accompanied by a governess and a tutor, they will live in Tantamount while their parents are on a sea voyage. Unknown to their father, the caretaker has so shamefully neglected Tantamount, that it is in a severe state of disrepair when the children and their chaperons arrive. The chaperons leave immediately, but the children choose to stay. Having been raised in a very proper Victorian household, the four Richleighs find great pleasure in their newfound freedom, and they quickly develop a self-reliance they had not known before. Together with two children who live alone in a cottage nearby, they discover the joys of sharing and of living a simple, unfettered life. Gradually too, they learn the unhappy secret that for years has given the castle an aura of evil and strikes fear in those who live in the surrounding countryside.

STORM FROM THE WEST. Illus. by Douglas Hall. New York: Harcourt, 1964. 189p.

When Robert Graham, an American, and Sarah Lattimer, an Englishwoman, decide to be married they know that there are more than the routine problems to be solved. Robert Graham has a family of four, and Sarah has a teen-age son and daughter. Bringing the two families together and molding them into one poses many problems before their summer in Scotland is over. The first meeting of the two families is somewhat strained, but is tempered by everyone's awareness of the need for harmony. The weeks pass with changing waves of emotion among them—reserve, friendliness, anger, and happiness. Everyone tries, but their life together—with all of its difficult adjustments—has to reach a climax before they can understand and accept each other, their family relationships, and their family customs. As the summer comes to a close, harmony seems assured.

Miss Willard has created a story brimming with human understanding, pathos, and humor.

THREE AND ONE TO CARRY. Illus. by Douglas Hall. New York: Harcourt, 1964. 186p. o.p.

Shortly after World War II, the Lodge family moves to Winterpicks, a small, neglected farm that Mr. Lodge hopes to make into a prosperous market garden. He manages to keep the family going, but there are numerous small disasters, and then the tragedy of their mother's death. Rosanna, the seventeen-year-old, firmly announces that she will be the housekeeper. Warmhearted and loving, she is forever bringing stray pets home to care for, but when she brings Arthur to Winterpicks, Prue and Tiger really protest. Arthur is a neglected and undisciplined boy, anything but a welcomed addition to the family. Life at Winterpicks becomes even more complicated when Arthur breaks his leg and Mr. Lodge is threatened with the loss of a part of the farm that the family loves. They all turn detectives in search of an old map that will prove the land's ownership, and Arthur in his bumbling way helps to find it.

An entertaining and fast moving story that will interest boys and girls in the middle grades.

THE LARK AND THE LAUREL. New York: Harcourt, 1970. 207p.

THE SPRIG OF BROOM. New York: Harcourt, 1972. 184p.

A COLD WIND BLOWING. New York: Harcourt, 1973. 175p.

THE IRON LILY. New York: Harcourt, 1974. 176p.

These four superior historical novels are a chronicle of generations of family living at Mantlemas, a country manor, from the end of the Wars of the Roses to the reign of Elizabeth I. Each book is an absorbing story of its own. In each, there is romance and mystery, rich historical background, strong characterization, and a skillful presentation of life as it was lived long ago. Together the books represent some of the best writing this author has done. They are all for the mature reader.

DATE DUE